Workbook

D0646189

Healing & Wellness

Your 10-Day Spiritual Action Plan

KENNETH
COPELAND
PUBLICATIONS

Kenneth & Gloria Copeland

Unless otherwise noted, all scripture is from the *King James Version* of the Bible.

Scripture quotations marked *The Amplified Bible* are from *The Amplified Bible, Old Testament* © 1965, 1987 by The Zondervan Corporation. *The Amplified New Testament* © 1958, 1987 by The Lockman Foundation. Used by permission.

Scripture quotations marked *New King James Version* are from the *New King James Version* © 1982 by Thomas Nelson Inc.

Scripture quotations marked *New International Version* are from *The Holy Bible, New International Version* © 1973, 1978, 1984 by the International Bible Society. Used by permission of Zondervan Publishing House.

Scripture quotations marked *Weymouth* are from *The New Testament in Modern Speech* by Richard Francis Weymouth © 1996 Kenneth Copeland Publications.

Includes material from *And Jesus Healed Them All*, the *Believer's Voice of Victory* magazine, *Blessed Beyond Measure, God's Prescription for Divine Health, Harvest of Health, How to Receive Communion, One Word From God Can Change Your Health, Declaration of Faith* brochure, *Walking in the Realm of the Miraculous, The Power of the Tongue, Know Your Enemy* and *You Are Healed!*, as well as newly created content and interactive action plans inspired by these resources.

Copyright information for *Healing Praise:*
"Give Thanks," Henry Smith, © 1978 Integrity's Hosanna! Music Inc., ASCAP • "Jesus Healed Them All," Steve Ingram, © 1991 Psalmist Covenant Music, ASCAP • "Only Believe," Paul Rader, © 1921 Public Domain • "'Tis So Sweet to Trust in Jesus," Louisa M.R. Stead, William J. Kirkpatrick, Public Domain • "I Sing Praises to Your Name," Terry MacAlmon, © 1989 Integrity's Hosanna! Music • "I Stand in Awe of You," Mark Altrogge, © 1988 People of Destiny Int./Pleasant Hill Music (Music Services) • "Nothing But the Blood," Robert Lowry, Public Domain • "O the Blood," Public Domain
• "Praise the Name of Jesus," Roy Hicks Jr., © 1976 Latter Rain Music (Admin. by EMICMG) • "More Precious Than Silver," Lynn DeShazo, © 1982 Integrity's Hosanna! Music • "O Come Let Us Adore Him," John Francis Wade, Public Domain • "There Is a Way," David Stearman, © 1987 Straightway Music (Admin. by EMICMG) • "All-Consuming Fire," Randy Wright, © 1987 Integrity's Hosanna! Music • "Sing Hallelujah," Linda Strassen Benjamin, © 1974
Linda Strassen, New Song Ministries • "Rise and Be Healed," Milton Bourgeois, © 1972 John T. Benson Publishing Co. (ASCAP) (Admin. by Brentwood-Benson Music Publishing Inc.) Music Services

Healing & Wellness

Your 10-Day Spiritual Action Plan

ISBN 978-1-60683-357-5   30-3000/30-3004
16 15 14 13 12 11   5 4 3 2 1

© 2008 Eagle Mountain International Church Inc. aka Kenneth Copeland Publications
Kenneth Copeland Publications
Fort Worth, TX 76192-0001

For more information about Kenneth Copeland Ministries, call 800-600-7395 or visit www.kcm.org.

All rights reserved under International Copyright Law. No part of this book may be reproduced or transmitted in any form or by any means, electronic or mechanical, including photocopying, recording, or by any information storage and retrieval system, without the written permission of the publisher.

Table of Contents

Quick-Start Guide

If you need healing now, here is a **Quick-Start Guide** to follow.

God sent His Word to heal you, and He always keeps His Word. His Word works!

Your healing may be instant or it may take some time before you can see and feel the total, physical effects of God's healing power. So, just because you don't see immediate results, do not let doubts and lingering symptoms discourage you. After all, when you go to a doctor, do you immediately feel better? No, the medication given to you usually takes some time before it begins to work. In the same way, the effects of divine healing may not appear instantly, either. It may take time for you to *feel* completely healed.

So, what do you do in the meantime? Exercise your faith! Here's how:

1. Make God's Word the final authority.

The Word says that by the stripes of Jesus you *were* healed (1 Peter 2:24).

2. Refuse to believe what you see and feel.

Only believe the Word.

3. Refuse doubt and unbelief.

When the devil whispers doubt and unbelief into your mind, deal with those thoughts immediately. Cast them down; don't dwell on them.

4. Meditate on God's Word.

Keep your mind fixed on the promises.

5. Cast your care on the Lord.

The devil will try to use anxiety over your situation to choke the Word out of your heart so the promises will become unfruitful (Mark 4:19).

6. Praise God for your healing!

Praising God before you see a manifestation is the highest form of faith.

7. Don't waver.

James said that the person who wavers in his faith should not expect to receive anything from the Lord (James 1:6-7).

8. Never let go!

No matter what happens, continue to stand on God's Word for your healing.

9. Listen to the Word!

One of the main methods of keeping your mind renewed to the Word is to listen to it on audio or video resources like CD or DVD.

10. Confess the Word concerning your healing.

It is difficult to believe you have received your healing if you are constantly talking about your sickness. Speak only words that are in agreement with God's will for your healing.

Your Healing Prayer and Confession

"Heavenly Father, I thank You for Your Word which says that by the stripes of Jesus I was healed. I choose to believe Your healing power went to work in my body the instant hands were laid on me (or the moment I believed Your Word).

"I confess Jesus Christ as Lord over my life—spirit, soul and body. I have received the power of God to make me sound, whole, delivered, saved and healed.

"Sickness, disease and pain, I resist you in the Name of Jesus. You are not the will of God for my life. I enforce the Word of God on you. I will not tolerate you in my life. My days of sickness and disease are over!

"Jesus bore my sickness, weakness and pain. I am forever free!

"Father, thank You for watching over Your Word to perform it in my behalf. I praise You and bless You in Jesus' Name!"

Your Healing Promises

- Isaiah 53:4-5
- Psalm 91:9-10, 14-16
- Psalm 103:1-5
- Jeremiah 30:17
- John 10:10

You will find more prayers, confessions and healing scriptures listed in the back of this book.

How to Use
Your LifeLine Kit

How to Use
Your LifeLine Kit

We believe this *Healing & Wellness: Your 10-day Spiritual Action Plan* will change your circumstances. It's our prayer that you experience *life* like never before—full, complete, strong and healthy in God. To accomplish this, we've created one of the most in-depth resources Kenneth Copeland Ministries has ever made available on this subject—all in one place! Here are some practical tips to get started and to help you make the most of this kit:

- Commit to making the next 10 days *your* days for renewing your mind. Set aside any distractions and be prepared to make adjustments in your life so you can get the most out of this kit.

- This plan should be a blessing, not a burden. If you miss a day or can't quite get through one day's materials, at your next opportunity, just start where you left off. If you have to, be flexible with the kit to ensure you make it to the end. If you only have one-half hour a day, that's fine—commit to that! It may take a little longer to complete the kit, but you can be confident you'll experience some of the most life-changing days you've ever had.

- Use this LifeLine workbook as your starting point each day to guide your reading, listening, watching and journaling. Before you know it, you'll be saturating your life with God's Word like never before.

- We recommend that you:

> **Read and journal** in the morning 📑✏️
> **Meditate** on the scriptures daily ✋
> **Watch** the video in the evening ◉
> **Read and journal** again at night 📑✏️

Remember, the goal is to do just a little every day. Steady doses are the best medicine.

Points to remember:

- This is an action book! Have a pen handy for underlining and taking notes.
- Fully engage with all the materials. Write in your workbook, speak the scriptures, pray the prayers, sing with the music and take time to enjoy the materials in every way.
- Carry your daily action card and refer to it throughout the day as a connecting point with God.
- Make your study time focused. Do your best to remove distractions and find a quiet place.

Your total healing and wellness are closer than ever! God loves you and He is for you. We are standing with you, and remember that "Jesus Is Lord!"

Chapter One
God's Will Is Healing

God Wants You Well!

by Gloria Copeland

And he came down with them, and stood in the plain, and the company of his disciples, and a great multitude of people out of all Judaea and Jerusalem, and from the sea coast of Tyre and Sidon, which came to hear him, and to be healed of their diseases; and they that were vexed with unclean spirits: and they were healed. And the whole multitude sought to touch him: for there went virtue out of him, and healed them all. (Luke 6:17-19)

God does not play favorites. It is His will for you to be healed. Period.

Now, you may hear me say that God wants you well and want to believe it—but your faith cannot operate beyond your knowledge of His Word. That's a large part of what this study is about: getting the Word inside you concerning healing.

God's Word says, "My people are destroyed for lack of knowledge..." (Hosea 4:6). In the physical realm this is true. The bodies of born-again believers are being destroyed because they do not have the knowledge of God's Word that it is His will for them to be healed. Many die young even though it is not God's will. God said, "I will take sickness away from the midst of thee.... The number of thy days I will fulfil" (Exodus 23:25-26). He says in Psalm 91:16, "With long life will I satisfy him, and show him my salvation." It is not His will for you to die young. It is His will for you to live long and satisfied on the earth without sickness and disease!

Healing is not just a New Testament blessing. God has always provided healing for His people. Psalm 103:2-3 says, "Bless the Lord, O my soul, and forget not all his benefits: who forgiveth all thine iniquities; who healeth all thy diseases."

Many have forgotten God's benefit of healing for their bodies. If you had been taught that it is God's will to heal you the same way you have been taught it is God's will for you to be saved, you would have a different attitude toward sickness. Jesus bore your sicknesses and carried your diseases at the same time and in the same manner that He bore your sins. You are just as free from sickness and disease as you are from sin. You should be as quick to refuse sickness and disease in your body as you are to refuse sin.

Plant the Word

To live free from sickness, you must plant the Word of God concerning healing in your heart. We'll be doing that throughout the 10 sessions in this workbook. God's Word is the incorruptible seed. First Peter 1:23 says you are "born again, not of corruptible seed, but of incorruptible, by the word of God, which liveth and abideth for ever." You are healed the same way— by the incorruptible seed of the Word of God. *Incorruptible* means that "the seed cannot be destroyed or spoiled." Disease cannot stop it. Men cannot spoil it. Satan cannot stop the power of it. I can prove that to you with salvation. Once you hear the Word of God and decide to make Jesus Christ the Lord of your life, there is no power that can stop the new birth from taking place in your spirit. No devil in hell can stop you from being born again. It is the same way with healing. You receive everything from the Lord the same way—by faith. Results come when you hear the Word, receive it and act on it. You receive healing exactly the way you received the new birth: by hearing the Word and believing it enough to act on it.

You have to put the supernatural seed of the Word of God in your heart. Plant it and it will grow and produce fruit. When you're dealing with God, His time is always *now*. He doesn't have to wait 60 days to get a crop. When you plant the Word in your heart, you get the harvest. *Today* is the day of salvation.

Your Power of Authority

Some people accept sickness as God's will. Yet, the same people will take medicine, be operated on, or do anything else they can in order to get well.

Christianity is not just on Sunday morning. Spiritual things work every day of the week. The Bible makes sense because it works! It works on Monday just like it does on Sunday. It is God's wisdom written in man's words, so that we can be victorious every day of the week.

Some people say, "Well, maybe God doesn't put sickness on you, but He allows Satan to do it." There is only one person who allows Satan to put sickness on you, and that's you.

As a believer, you have authority in the earth over Satan, sickness and disease. If sickness has come upon you, you have allowed it, not God. God doesn't have to allow Satan to make you sick. Satan is always ready to do the job! Sickness incapacitates you and makes you no threat to him at all.

You need to lay aside what tradition has taught you and realize that only Satan could be the source of such powerless, defeated beliefs. The Word of God is the incorruptible seed. If Satan does not have the power to stop it and disease cannot overcome it, then only you have the power to keep it from working in your life.

As you study the incorruptible seed of the Word of God in this LifeLine kit, keep your mind and spirit open to the Word to change your thinking. Doubt and unbelief will try to come against you and say, "Now, you know what they say about all this...." Who are "they"? Well, "they" will be the ones who bury you early if you listen to their traditions. Cast out the doubt and keep the Word.

Receive the Word of God. The power

and blessing you receive from it will be according to how you hear it. You must receive it as God talking to you, as the Word of the living God and the authority in your life. You must decide that whatever you see in it, you'll act on. If you just receive a little here and a little there, thinking, *Well, now, that could be true...,* you'll get nothing from it. But, when you allow the incorruptible seed to go into your heart, it *will* produce the crop you desire...every time!

(From: *And Jesus Healed Them All* by Gloria Copeland © 1981 International Church of the Word of Faith Inc. now known as Eagle Mountain International Church aka Kenneth Copeland Publications)

Morning Reflection

How are salvation and healing related?

_____

_____

_____

_____

What must you do to live free from sickness and disease?

_____

_____

_____

_____

How will you commit to changing your thinking in this area?

_____

_____

_____

_____

Today's Connection Points

⊙ *Healing Praise* **CD: "There Is a Way" (Track 9)**

Healing may seem impossible right now, but as you focus on today's track, feed your spirit with the truth that *there is a way!*

⊙ *Healing Scriptures* CD: Tracks 1-2

Feed your spirit over and over with these powerful scriptures, proving that God's will is for you to be healed.

> 1 Corinthians 3:21-23; Proverbs 4:20-22; Exodus
> 15:26; Psalm 103:1-3, 107:19-20;
> Isaiah 53:3-5; Matthew 4:23-24, 8:2-3, 5-8, 13, 16-17, 9:18-30, 35

⊙ DVD: "Great Is the Lord" (Chapter 1)

Listening to the Word about healing will strengthen your faith! Watch as Gloria talks about the Lord's greatness and His ability to heal as we believe we receive.

Faith in Action

✋ *Realize that God wants you well!*
Commit to studying the Word like never before and allow it to change your way of thinking.

Notes:

_____

_____

_____

_____

_____

_____

_____

_____

_____

_____

_____

_____

_____

_____

"I Want My People Well"
by Kenneth Copeland

Sometime ago, God dealt with me on the subject of healing and how important it is for believers to live free from sickness and disease. His words to me then were so strong, they echoed in my spirit for weeks. He said, *I want My people well!*

God wants every believer to be healed and whole. He says in 3 John 2, "Beloved, I wish above all things that thou mayest prosper and be in health, even as thy soul prospereth."

After Jesus was raised from the dead, He appeared to His disciples and issued certain decrees that would affect the world forever. Healing was one of those decrees. Jesus said:

> Go ye into all the world, and preach the gospel to every creature. He that believeth and is baptized shall be saved; but he that believeth not shall be damned. And these signs shall follow them that believe; In my name shall they cast out devils; they shall speak with new tongues; they shall take up serpents; and if they drink any deadly thing, it shall not hurt them; they shall lay hands on the sick, and they shall recover (Mark 16:15-18).

These words are vitally important to every believer today. Jesus commanded the Church to go forth in His Name, and part of this Great Commission is that believers lay hands on the sick. At that moment, Jesus set the Church against sickness and disease.

Healing is God's masterstroke of evidence that He is alive and doing well. It is physical proof of His existence and willingness to meet our needs on every level.

Spiritual Maturity

No two people are exactly the same spiritually. Each is at his individual level of spiritual growth. But generally, there are three categories of spiritual life:

1. The world—sinners or unbelievers, who do not know God
2. The carnally minded Christian —spiritual babies, who do not have God's Word working proficiently in their lives
3. The mature Christian— spiritual adults, skillful in the Word of God

God's Word is designed to minister to individual needs at each level of spiritual growth. In 1 Corinthians 3:1-3,

Paul refers to the two levels of spiritual maturity within the Body of Christ, the Church: "And I, brethren, could not speak unto you as unto spiritual, but as unto carnal, even as unto babes in Christ. I have fed you with milk, and not with meat: for hitherto ye were not able to bear it, neither yet now are ye able. For ye are yet carnal: for whereas there is among you envying, and strife, and divisions, are ye not carnal, and walk as men?"

Paul could not teach the Corinthian believers about deeper spiritual things because they were not mature enough to understand. They were "babes in Christ," and he had to feed them with "milk"—the basic principles of faith—as you would feed a tiny baby. Hebrews 5:13 says, "For every one that useth milk is unskilful in the word of righteousness: for he is a babe." First Peter 2:2 says, "As newborn babes, desire the sincere milk of the word, that ye may grow thereby."

When you accepted Jesus as Savior and made Him the Lord of your life, you were "born of God" (1 John 5:1). According to 1 Peter 1:23, you were "born again," not of corruptible seed, but of incorruptible, by the Word of God. At that moment, you joined the family of God and entered into spiritual life as a newborn baby. If, since that time, you have never fed on the milk of the Word, you are still a spiritual baby. You will not yet be able to operate proficiently in faith without knowledge of the Word.

A baby does not grow to adulthood overnight, so a new believer should not expect to operate as a mature Christian after only a few days. It takes time spent in God's Word to grow and mature spiritually.

The first step to spiritual maturity is to realize your position in God. You are His child and a joint heir with Jesus. Romans 8:16-17 says: "The Spirit itself beareth witness with our spirit, that we are the children of God: and if children, then heirs; heirs of God, and joint-heirs with Christ; if so be that we suffer with him, that we may be also glorified together." You are entitled to all the rights and privileges in the kingdom of God, and one of these rights is health and healing.

You will never fully realize nor understand healing until you know beyond any doubt that God's will is for you to be healed. As we have seen, God wants you healed! He wants you whole! He wants you to grow in the Word and walk in His perfect will just as Jesus did. Whether or not you accept this and purpose to walk in the reality of the truth is your decision.

I urge you to accept it now and begin to see His will carried out in your life. Begin seeing yourself healed and whole. Put God's Word concerning healing in your heart, meditate, or think about it, then speak it out boldly. His Word will not return to Him void, but it will accomplish what it was sent to do (Isaiah 55:11). Praise God!

(From: *You Are Healed*, by Kenneth Copeland © 1979 Eagle Mountain International Church Inc. aka Kenneth Copeland Publications)

Evening Reflection

How does the Great Commission reflect God's will toward healing?

_____
_____
_____
_____
_____
_____

What does God's healing power demonstrate to the world?

_____
_____
_____
_____
_____

How will understanding God's will about healing increase your spiritual maturity?

_____
_____
_____
_____
_____

Notes:

_____
_____
_____
_____
_____
_____

Today's Prayer of Faith

Thank You, Father, that I am born again by the incorruptible seed of the Word of God and free from the law of sin and death! I choose to live by Your Word, and I trust You to help me grow and mature. In Jesus' Name. Amen.

REAL-LIFE TESTIMONIES
To Help Build Your Faith

No More Pain

Two years ago I was in a car accident that left me in a lot of pain. There was also an injury to my spine. After eight months of pain, lack of sleep, nausea and the inability to care for my family, God told me to listen to Gloria's healing CDs. I played them repeatedly and listened to them as I drifted in and out of sleep. As the days went by, I was able to sleep more and more. I was able to stand longer and the pain lessened. Ten days later, when I went to the doctor, he verified that my spine was healed. We have continued to see amazing things God has done. Thank you for your ministry.

C.V.
Wisconsin

Chapter Two
Understanding the Battle

The Cost of Tradition
by Gloria Copeland

Faith should be as highly developed in the Church concerning healing as it is for the new birth of the spirit. If the Church had been told what the Word says about healing, Christians would be as quick to believe they are healed as they are to believe they are saved. However, other things have been sown in our hearts. Seeds of doubt and unbelief have been sown by the traditions of men who try to teach the Word with head knowledge instead of by His Spirit.

God's Word doesn't make sense to the carnal mind. Men try to explain it through their own natural thinking, but they never succeed. Because they have no revelation knowledge of the Word, men in pulpits across our nation have preached things that are simply not true. Traditions cost people the healing power of God. Jesus said the traditions of men make the Word of no effect (Matthew 15:6). Perhaps you've even believed some of these fallacies.

Tradition, Tradition, Tradition

One tradition that has robbed the Church of healing is the practice of praying, "If it be Thy will." You should know it is God's will to heal you before you ever pray. You can know because God's Word tells you His will. The Word of God is the will of God. "If it be Thy will" is unbelief when praying for healing. There is no faith in that kind of prayer. It is the opposite of faith. If you are praying, "Lord, heal me, if it be Thy will," then it is obvious that you don't know what the will of God is, and until you know, you don't have any basis for faith. But you can know God's will—it's in His Word.

Another tradition we have heard is that healing has passed away, and miracles don't happen today. We all know that God doesn't change (James 1:17). He has not changed since the beginning of time (Malachi 3:6). He said, "I am the Lord that healeth thee" (Exodus 15:26). For healing to have passed away, God would have to pass away. He is still the Lord who heals us!

Miracles and the healing power of God are just as available now as when Jesus walked the earth. You can believe that God heals today. Miracles have never passed away—some people just quit believing. It takes active faith to receive from God.

There was a time in my life when I knew that healing was real and that God is still healing people today, but I didn't know if it was God's will to heal *me*. Just believing in healing is not enough. You must believe that it is God's will to heal *you*. You have to believe that healing is yours, that it belongs to you.

Another tradition tells us that God gets glory from Christians being sick. But the Bible says people gave glory to God when they saw the lame walk and blind eyes see. People glorified the God of Israel when they saw His power in manifestation (Matthew 15:30-31). Jesus said the Father is glorified when we bear much fruit (John 15:8). Cancer is not fruit. Arthritis is not fruit. The world is not impressed by your sickness. They are not impressed because you bear up under pain and agony. They have all the pain and agony they want. They are looking for a way out of sickness and disease—not a way into it. They have enough problems. They want answers! People are oppressed by Satan and need deliverance. They want victory in their lives. They want to know how to pay their bills and be free of sickness in their bodies. That God gets glory from His children being sick makes no sense; but more important, it does not agree with the Word of God.

As believers, we are to be lighthouses of deliverance and help in a dark world. God's will is that we show forth His love and power to the hurting world around us. The Bible says, "Let your light so shine before men, that they may see your good works, and glorify your Father which is in heaven" (Matthew 5:16).

The world is supposed to see good works in our midst, not sickness and disease. "That ye may be blameless and harmless, the sons of God, without rebuke, in the midst of a crooked and perverse nation, among whom ye shine as lights in the world; holding forth the word of life" (Philippians 2:15-16). Our commission is to give forth the Word of life—the Word of God concerning salvation, healing and deliverance to those around us. Instead, because of the traditions of men, we have tried to tell the world that the God we serve has made us sick. What a lie to tell about the Father God who is the God of love and mercy! Jesus said that we are to lay hands on the sick and they would recover. His will is that His Body, the believers, be the answer to the problem of sickness and disease. We have been told by Him to alleviate the problem. Teaching people that God wants them sick only adds to it.

Paul's Thorn in the Flesh

Another tradition that has been well taught is referred to as Paul's "thorn in the flesh" from 2 Corinthians 12. Everyone seems to have heard about it. Tradition teaches that Paul's thorn in the flesh was sickness or disease, but the Word plainly says that the thorn was a "messenger of Satan." In the New Testament, this Greek word is translated *messenger* seven times and *angel* 181 times.

All 188 times this word is speaking of a personality—not a thing like a sickness or disease. Sickness is not a messenger, nor is it a personality. Satan sent an angel or messenger to Paul to buffet him. The word *buffet* means "to give repeated blows, over and over and over." Weymouth's translation says, "Concerning this, three times have I besought the Lord that *he* might leave me" (2 Corinthians 12:8). The *King*

James Version says, "For this thing I besought the Lord thrice, that it might depart from me." The thorn in the flesh was not a sickness as tradition teaches, but a messenger from Satan, as the Bible teaches. God does not use Satan's messenger service. God did not give Paul this thorn in the flesh—Satan sent Paul the thorn to stop the Word from being preached.

The terms "thorn in the flesh" or "thorn in the side" are always used as *illustrations* in the Bible. For example, the Lord told Moses that if the Israelites did not drive out the inhabitants of the land of Canaan, they would become "pricks in [their] eyes, and thorns in [their] sides..." (Numbers 33:55). The Canaanites were not sticking in to the Israelites' sides! This is just an illustration. Today, we still use the term "a thorn in the flesh." Your neighbor might be a "thorn" in your side. In the same way we say, "That guy is a pain in the neck." Tradition says this thorn was something in Paul's actual flesh, but 2 Corinthians 12:7 is the same type of illustration. Weymouth's translation of this verse says, "...there was given me a thorn in the flesh, *Satan's angel* to torture me." This evil spirit was assigned to Paul in order to stop the Word. Jesus said in Mark 4 that Satan comes immediately to steal the Word. Paul was having to stand against this evil spirit everywhere he went.

When Paul asked God to do something about this messenger of Satan, the Lord said, "My grace is sufficient for thee..." (2 Corinthians 12:9). Tradition reads that he asked the Lord to deliver him and the Lord said no. Therefore, Paul had to endure the thorn forever. The Bible actually says, "And he said unto me, My grace is sufficient for thee: for my strength is made perfect in weakness." God was saying, "My favor is enough. You have authority. You have the Name of Jesus and when you're humanly weak, My strength or My power is made perfect."

We can see an excellent example of this in Acts 14, when Paul was stoned. He was dead, but the disciples gathered around him, prayed and the Lord raised him up. It was humanly impossible for him to do anything. In his own strength he had no ability to overcome, but when he was humanly weak, the power of God was strong.

In 2 Corinthians 12:10, Paul wrote, "Therefore I take pleasure in infirmities, in reproaches, in necessities, in persecutions, in distresses for Christ's sake...." Let's look over these words. *Infirmity* means "want of strength, weakness, indicating inability to produce results." It does not mean sickness. It means what the Lord said: "When your strength ends, My power is made perfect." The other things mentioned here—reproaches, necessities, persecutions, distresses—are the buffetings Paul lists in 2 Corinthians 11. He was imprisoned, stoned, beaten, shipwrecked and attacked by angry mobs. Sickness is not mentioned.

We have heard a lot about trials and tribulations that came on Paul, but tradition forgets to mention that Satan's angel could gain no victory over Paul through adverse circumstances. Paul lived to be an old man. When it was time for him to go, he said he didn't know whether he wanted to stay or depart (Philippians 1:20-26). Paul did not go home to be with the Lord until he and the Lord were ready. He was a victorious Christian. He wrote most of the New Testament. He traveled throughout the known world. Satan's angel never could stop the Word of God from going forth.

Paul's own testimony was, "For I am now ready to be offered, and the time of my departure is at hand. I have fought a good fight, I have finished my course, I have kept the faith" (2 Timothy 4:6-7). That is not a description of a man who was sick or weak. Glory to God!

Paul was a victorious man. He said, "Persecutions, sufferings—such as occurred to me at Antioch, at Iconium, and at Lystra, persecutions I endured, but out of them all the Lord delivered me" (2 Timothy 3:11, *The Amplified Bible*). Tradition forgets to tell us that! Paul faced trials and tribulations, but the Lord delivered him out of them all! The thorn in the flesh that we have heard so much about could gain no victory over Paul and the Word of God. The messenger of Satan could only aggravate and harass Paul. He could not stop the Word from going forth. There is a big difference between being aggravated and being defeated! In every situation Paul faced, even death by stoning, the power of God was made strong and delivered him. This is teaching that the Church needs to hear: When human strength ends, the power of God excels!

You can see how helpless we have been with traditions planted in our hearts and minds, instead of God's Word. You cannot stand in faith against sickness and disease when you have been taught that sickness is God's will for you. How can you stand in faith for your healing when you think God has put cancer on you to teach you something? This tradition is an abomination to the nature of God! God wants you healed. Despite what tradition says, *that's* the truth!

(From: *And Jesus Healed Them All* by Gloria Copeland © 1981 International Church of the Word of Faith Inc. now known as Eagle Mountain International Church aka Kenneth Copeland Publications)

Morning Reflection

What traditions have you grown up believing?

_____
_____
_____
_____
_____
_____
_____
_____

What does the Bible *really* tell us about Paul's thorn in the flesh?

_____

_____

_____

_____

_____

_____

_____

How have traditions hindered the Church?

_____

_____

_____

_____

_____

_____

_____

_____

Today's
Connection Points

- ● *Healing Praise* **CD: "Only Believe" (Track 3)**

  Put aside traditions today as you focus on "Only Believe"—that all things are possible.

- ● *Healing Scriptures* **CD: Track 7**

  Jesus paid for our healing—spirit, soul and body. Hear how He has given you LIFE!

  John 10:10, 11:17-45

- ● **DVD: "Bless the Lord" (Chapter 2)**

  Don't forget His benefits! Watch as Gloria ministers on the One who heals *all* our diseases.

Challenge the traditions you've been taught about healing.

God isn't the source of sickness; He's your healer!

Notes:

_____

_____

_____

_____

_____

_____

_____

_____

_____

_____

_____

_____

_____

_____

_____

_____

_____

The Troublemaker
by Kenneth Copeland

When we were in Mexico, I went to a bullfight that left a lasting impression on me: The bull didn't know who his enemy was. He thought that red cape was his enemy. I remember thinking, *If he ever realized his* real *source of trouble, that matador wouldn't have a chance.*

As I travel among Christians everywhere, it is very evident to me that many believers are just like that poor bull. They are battling "red capes" instead of getting to the real source of their problems. They are contending against the trouble instead of *the troublemaker.*

Who is the troublemaker? Who is the real source of all of your troubles, whether they are spiritual, mental, physical, social or financial? If you knew, you would no longer struggle against the "red cape" of your problems. You would eliminate the very source of them. Just as that matador was no match for that mean, ferocious bull, the troublemaker is no match for the believer who battles him with the full armor and mighty weapons of God.

When sickness or trouble arises, the most natural thing to do is to place the blame for it on someone or something. Sadly, for the most part, many Christians have been falsely accusing God of being the cause of their troubles. This is the No. 1 deception sown in the Church today: that our problems, our sicknesses and our temptations are sent by God to teach us. This lie says that trials and tribulations are God's tools for developing and strengthening our character. The extreme end of this deception is that God Himself is the author of our troubles or that He is the one who makes us sick in order to teach us something.

This is absolutely against the Word of God. Why? Because the very basic principle of the Christian life is to know that God put our sin, sickness, disease, sorrow, grief and poverty on Jesus at Calvary. For God to put any of this on us now to teach us or to strengthen our faith would be a miscarriage of justice. To believe that God has a purpose for your sickness would mean that Jesus bore your sickness in vain. What an insult to His love and care and compassion toward you!

In order to place blame where it is due, we need a fresh revelation of who our true source of trouble is. The only way we will receive this revelation is by rightly dividing the Word of Truth. James 1:8 says that a double-minded man is unstable in all his ways, and Jesus said in Luke 11:17 that a house divided against itself will fall. Therefore, if a man thinks, imagines, assumes, or in any way has the idea that God is behind his trouble—either by permission or commission—he will never resist it. And if he doesn't resist it, then he will certainly fail because his hesitation will give Satan just the edge he needs to defeat him.

In the world of the spirit, there is a challenger, a counterfeit, an opponent of God who knows his business. But there is also the armor of God, the Word of God, and the power it takes to defeat this opponent. The Word says to resist Satan, and he will flee from you. But when a man is in a hesitating area—not opposing, but wondering—then Satan can easily defeat him. We must clearly distinguish between what is coming from Satan and not blame God for something He's not behind. This is why it's extremely important to rightly divide the Word concerning this issue.

The Dividing Line

John 10:10 is the dividing line between life and death. The thief, Satan, comes only to steal, kill and destroy. Jesus came that we might have life and have it more abundantly.

Satan is the thief. He is trying to rob the Body of Christ of its power. The believer has the whole armor of God available to him, and Satan has no defense for that armor. Instead, he must deceive the believer and sidetrack him. He must operate in the world of the natural because in the world of the spirit, the believer can beat him with his powerful spiritual weapons. The sword of the Spirit, God's Word, can wound

Satan deeply, so he uses deception. He comes against the believer in the physical world and tries to convince him that God is actually the one who made him sick or that God took his baby or that God wants him to live in poverty. If the believer entertains those thoughts for any length of time, he will begin to doubt. He will hesitate. He will become double-minded. That hesitation will give Satan a valuable advantage. Then the next time he attacks, the believer will be a little easier to defeat.

The believer must decide not to back up any longer. The man who is single-minded on God's Word has to know for sure that God's will was Jesus on the cross and that God's will is for him to prosper and be in health. He must know God's will is to meet all his needs according to His riches in glory by Christ Jesus and for him to receive the blessings of Abraham through faith in Jesus Christ. When these facts become a reality on the inside of him, then he becomes a powerful believer, a joint heir with Jesus Christ. He knows that his Father has carefully planned for his deliverance and victory. From that point forward, he'll never question whether or not he should prosper or whether or not he ought to be healed. He is no longer on the defensive—he is on the attack. He no longer hesitates—he is constant and stable.

Jesus said He would build His Church on the rock and the gates of hell would not prevail against it, or in other words, the powers of hell would not succeed against it (Matthew 16:18). That rock is the Word of God. Jesus likened the man who acts on the Word to a man who built his house on a rock (Luke 6:48-49). When the storm beat vehemently against the house, it stood strong. You see, in this parable the same storm beat against both houses—the one on the rock and the one on the sand. It wasn't the storm that made the house strong. The house was strong *before* the storm hit. It was built on a firm foundation. This is how the Body of Christ is to be—built on the firm foundation of the Word of God.

Become single-minded. Make the decision—choose life and blessing. Decide to win. Decide to overcome. Until this decision is made, you will be double-minded. But the moment you make your decision to be a winner, you will be out on top! There will be times when you'll have to stand and be patient and consistent, but when a man is consistent on the Word of God, he will know the truth and the truth will make him free.

(From: *Know Your Enemy* by Kenneth Copeland © 2002 Kenneth Copeland)

Evening Reflection

How is the enemy like a matador?

_____

_____

_____

_____

_____

_____

Why couldn't God use sickness to teach or strengthen us?

_____

_____

_____

_____

_____

_____

What does it mean to be single-minded on God's Word?

_____

_____

_____

_____

_____

_____

Notes:

_____
_____
_____
_____
_____
_____
_____
_____
_____
_____
_____
_____
_____
_____

Today's
Prayer of Faith

Father, I see how religious traditions, double-mindedness and discouragement can keep me from walking in Your life and health. But I choose life, and I know Your grace is sufficient for me. Your truth has made me free! Thank You, Lord! In Jesus' Name. Amen.

_____
_____
_____
_____
_____
_____
_____
_____
_____

God's Prescription Works

Years ago while under the influence of a denomination that did not believe in healing, I had a heart attack and stroke at the age of 40. After I got out of the hospital I was depleted, discouraged and disillusioned. My wife recorded one of your broadcasts on healing. I was hungry to understand what you were preaching. I knew if I could get it in my spirit, I would be free. As I pressed in, a boldness came into me as I talked to God and declared I was healed by the stripes of Jesus. Two and a half years later, I was checked over by Dr. Cherry to find I had a new heart and the blood pressure of an athlete.

For the past five years my wife and I have been going to churches in small, rural towns whose members are dying with disease. We have seen all kinds of miracles—people walking out of wheelchairs, ears opening, eyes seeing and the cripples healed.

Ever since we have been Partners with you, the number of churches we minister in has grown and the healing anointing has gotten stronger.

W.B.
North Carolina

Chapter Three
Healing in Redemption

He Bore Our Sicknesses

by Gloria Copeland

❝That it might be fulfilled which was spoken by Esaias the prophet, saying, Himself took our infirmities, and bare our sicknesses" (Matthew 8:17).

When Jesus bore our sins, He also bore our diseases. The Cross pronounced a complete cure for the ills of mankind. The Church has been made just as free from sickness as it has been made free from sin. Sure, a Christian may continue to sin after he has been born again, but he doesn't have to. Sin no longer has any rule over him unless he allows it (Romans 6:14). In the same way, a Christian may continue to be sick after he has been born again, but he does not have to be. He has been redeemed from sickness. The price has been paid for his healing. Sickness can no longer rule over him unless he allows it.

Most believers have only known a part of their redemption. Because their faith operates to the degree of their knowledge of God's Word, they find themselves sick time and again. They would have begun to live in divine health long ago if they had realized that healing belonged to them.

As you accept the fact that as surely as Jesus bore your sins, He also bore your diseases, weaknesses and pains, your days of sickness will be over. Understanding the truth of God's Word concerning healing will destroy Satan's grip on your life. The truth makes you free from his dominion when you realize that your healing has already been purchased. Isaiah 53:4-5 says, "Surely he hath borne our griefs, and carried our sorrows: yet we did esteem him stricken, smitten of God, and afflicted. But he was wounded for our transgressions, he was bruised for our iniquities: the chastisement of our peace was upon him; and with his stripes we are healed."

All of Isaiah 53 is about the substitution of Jesus for man. It says, "Surely he hath borne our griefs." *Young's Analytical Concordance to the Bible* says *choli,* translated "griefs," means "sickness, weakness and pain." Surely He has borne *your* sickness, weakness and pain! Think about that for a minute. Praise God!

Jesus was smitten with sin *and* sickness in order for you to be free from *both*. Verse 6 tells us, "The Lord hath laid on him the iniquity of us all." Verse 10 says, "Yet it pleased the Lord to bruise him; he hath put him to grief...." (According to Dr.

Young, the word *grief* means to "make sick" and should be translated, "He has made Him sick.")

What did Jesus do with your sickness? According to the Word, He bore it for you. It could not be God's will for you to be sick with the sickness that Jesus suffered for you. Because God so loved the world, He engineered the substitution of His only begotten Son to redeem man from the curse of Satan. Galatians 3:13 says, "Christ hath redeemed us from the curse of the law, being made a curse for us: for it is written, Cursed is every one that hangeth on a tree." Jesus was willing to take the curse in His own spirit, soul and body so that you would not have to continue under Satan's dominion.

There was no sickness before man became one with Satan at Adam's fall. Sin is the root from which sickness came. Just as sin is the manifestation of spiritual death in the heart of man, sickness is the manifestation of spiritual death in the body of man.

Not only did Jesus pay the price for the new birth of your spirit and the healing of your body, He also bore the chastisement of your peace. Satan has no right to torment you mentally. You have been redeemed from fear, mental anxiety, depression and anything else that keeps your mind from enjoying peace. You don't have to rely on drugs or pills. Jesus has already paid the price for you to be whole in your mind and enjoy peace. Do not allow Satan to steal your peace.

A Great Price

Jesus came to destroy the works of the devil—*all* of his works (1 John 3:8). He did not destroy sin only to leave sickness in dominion. Partial redemption from Satan's power would not have pleased God nor would it have fulfilled His plan for His family. He redeemed the *whole* man—righteousness for his nature, peace for his mind and healing for his body. Redemption left nothing in play that came on man as a result of sin. Jesus completely destroyed the works of the devil in our lives.

First Corinthians 6:20 says, "For ye are bought with a price." A great price! "Therefore glorify God in your body, and in your spirit, which are God's." There should not be any sickness in the Body of Christ. When someone around us is sick, God's healing power should flow so that he receives healing.

In the book of Leviticus, Israel used a scapegoat. The priest laid hands on a real goat, confessed the sins of the people on him and sent him into the wilderness— totally away from the people (Leviticus 16:21). That's what Jesus did with your sickness and disease! He bore them away from you! What you need to do is stand up in the Name of Jesus and command sickness and disease to go away from you. Give it no place in your body. Refuse to allow Satan to have any place in your body. Command sickness and disease to depart from your very presence—out of your home and your family.

The English language does not clearly communicate to us what the word *salvation* (the Greek word *sozo*) really means. It's not just the new birth of your spirit. It's also peace for your mind and healing for your body. *Vine's Expository Dictionary of Biblical Words* says salvation denotes "deliverance, preservation; material and temporal deliverance from danger and apprehension." Mark 16:15 says, "And he said unto them, Go ye into all the world, and preach the gospel to every creature." The gospel is the good news of what Jesus did for us—spirit, soul *and* body—and God wants us to let the world know!

There is no sin so great that Jesus' sacrifice at Calvary will not cancel it and wipe it away—as though sin had never been. The power of God cleanses and changes anyone who receives salvation until there is no trace of the old man or his sins. You become a new man, a new creature. Your new spirit is created in the righteousness of God.

In the same way, Jesus bore sickness away from you and by His stripes you were healed. That's a *fact*. There is no disease so devastating to the human body that the same sacrifice at Calvary will not cancel it and wipe it away, and heal your body—as though sickness had never been!

The gospel is the good news of what Jesus did for every person. He bore your sins, so you do not have to bear them. You can be forgiven, now! He did that for every sinner. He also bore your diseases, so you do not have to bear them. You can be healed, now! He did that for every sick man.

As the Body of Christ, we do not have to tolerate sickness or disease any longer. Jesus paid the price for our redemption from all the curse of the law. *All* of it.

(From: *And Jesus Healed Them All* by Gloria Copeland © 1981 International Church of the Word of Faith Inc. now known as Eagle Mountain International Church aka Kenneth Copeland Publications)

Morning Reflection

What does the Bible say that Jesus bore on the cross for us?

_____

_____

_____

_____

_____

_____

_____

_____

_____

_____

_____

_____

What price did Jesus pay for us to be healed, spirit, soul and body?

_____
_____
_____
_____
_____
_____
_____
_____
_____
_____
_____

What benefits are included in the biblical meaning of _salvation?_

_____
_____
_____
_____
_____
_____
_____
_____
_____

Today's Connection Points

- *Healing Praise* CD: "Nothing But the Blood of Jesus"/
"O, the Blood"/"Praise the Name of Jesus" (Medley) (Track 7)

Today's track focuses on the mighty blood of Jesus, and its redemptive work for your healing.

⊙ *Healing Scriptures* CD: Track 9

Jesus bore our sin and sickness on the cross. Strengthen your faith with these scriptures about redemption.

Acts 8:5-8, 9:32-42

⊙ DVD: "Psalm 91" (Chapter 3)

Watch, as Gloria talks about Psalm 91 and how God promises protection for the believer and victory from all sickness and disease.

✋ *Proclaim your complete redemption from sickness and disease.*

Receive righteousness for your nature, peace for your mind and healing for your body!

Notes:

_____
_____
_____
_____
_____
_____
_____
_____
_____
_____
_____
_____
_____
_____
_____
_____
_____
_____
_____

A Covenant of Healing

by Kenneth Copeland

Anytime a believer has a problem receiving healing, he usually suffers from ignorance of God's Word and ignorance of his rights and privileges in Jesus Christ. To fully understand your position, you need to realize what took place many centuries ago between God and a man named Abram. God approached Abram with a proposition. The agreement, or *covenant,* they made together is the basis of the entire New Testament. It was in behalf of this covenant that Jesus came to earth.

God's Covenant of Healing

Healing is not a new provision that came because of the ministry of Jesus. Healing was provided for under the Abrahamic covenant. This is how that covenant came into existence:

And when Abram was ninety years old and nine, the Lord appeared to Abram, and said unto him, I am the Almighty God; walk before me, and be thou perfect. And I will make my covenant between me and thee, and will multiply thee exceedingly. And Abram fell on his face: and God talked with him, saying, As for me, behold, my covenant is with

thee, and thou shalt be a father of many nations. Neither shall thy name any more be called Abram, but thy name shall be Abraham; for a father of many nations have I made the.... And I will establish my covenant between me and thee and thy seed after thee in their generations for an everlasting covenant, to be a God unto thee, and to thy seed after thee (Genesis 17:1-5, 7).

When God appeared to Abram He said, "I am the Almighty God." The original Hebrew says, "I am El Shaddai." *El* means "supreme." *Shaddai* means "the Breasty One." He said, "I will be a God to you." In other words, "I will be all you need—your father, your mother, your nurse, your provider."

Realize the full significance of what took place between God and Abraham. They entered into a contract together. They made covenant together—an everlasting covenant, an absolute agreement. God said, "As for me, behold, my covenant is with thee." Then He sealed His side of the agreement by swearing an oath. In Genesis 22:16, God said, "By myself have I sworn." There was no higher power to swear by, so He swore by Himself. He gave His own word that He would bless Abraham and his seed. He said, "That in blessing I will bless thee, and in multiplying I will multiply thy seed.... And in thy seed shall all the nations of the earth be blessed" (Genesis 22:17-18).

The Hebrew word *covenant* means "to cut," implying "where blood flows." A blood covenant is the strongest form of agreement on earth. Two parties agree to certain terms and then seal their agreement by the shedding of blood. The covenant made between God and Abraham was sealed through the act of circumcision. "This is my covenant, which ye shall keep, between me and you and thy seed after thee; every man child among you shall be circumcised. And ye shall circumcise the flesh of your foreskin; and it shall be a token of the covenant betwixt me and you" (Genesis 17:10-11).

The shedding of blood was the most vital act of the Old Testament. In circumcision, it stood as a sign of agreement, a token of the covenant between God and man. El Shaddai agreed to bless Abraham and his descendants exceedingly. In return, He required them to live uprightly before Him.

But man continually sinned against God, failing to hold to the terms of the agreement. Again, the shedding of blood held the answer. The Levitical priesthood was instituted to offer blood sacrifices that would atone (or cover) for sin. Without the shedding of blood, there is no remission of sin (Hebrews 9:22). By offering a lamb on the altar, the priests could purchase forgiveness for God's covenant people for one year. God accepted these sacrifices in order to keep the Abrahamic covenant in force.

This was the only way to bridge the gap between sin and righteousness.

Centuries later, the supreme blood sacrifice was made. Jesus of Nazareth came into the world, born of a virgin. When John the Baptist first saw Jesus, he said, "Behold the Lamb of God, which taketh away the sin of the world" (John 1:29). Jesus was the sacrificial lamb offered on the altar of the cross. He was the final sacrifice of the Levitical priesthood. The blood He shed on the cross washed away, forever, the spot of sin. The Old Testament sacrifices only *covered* sin. The New Testament sacrifice—Jesus, the spotless Son of God—completely did away with it. Hebrews 9:12 says, "Neither by the blood of goats and calves, but by his own blood he entered in once into the holy place, having obtained eternal redemption for us." By accepting His sacrifice, you stand before God clean and pure—just as if you had never sinned.

Jesus bore the penalty of sin and, at the same time, did away with all the effects of it. When sin entered the world, it brought with it the forces of destruction: death, sickness, poverty and fear. The price Jesus paid at Calvary was the full price, covering every area of human life: spiritual, mental, physical, financial and social. Our redemption is complete.

Galatians 3:13-14 says, "Christ hath redeemed us from the curse of the law, being made a curse for us: for it is written, Cursed is every one that hangeth on a tree: that the blessing of Abraham might come on the Gentiles through Jesus Christ; that we might receive the promise of the Spirit through faith."

"The curse of the Law" is described in Deuteronomy 28:15. It was the penalty for any person who disobeyed the statutes of the Levitical Law. It included every possible curse that could come on mankind: sickness, disease, poverty, lack, pain, suffering, etc. Then verse 61 includes, "Also every sickness, and every plague, which is not written in the book of this law...."

Though Jesus lived a sinless life, He gave Himself to bear that curse as if He had sinned and disobeyed the Law. He took the punishment for the sin of mankind. He bore the curse which included every sickness and every plague known to man. He bore pain and suffering. Why? So we could receive the *blessing* when we accept His sacrifice as our own. Because we are in Christ, we are now Abraham's seed and heirs to the blessing.

Galatians 3:29 says, "And if ye be Christ's, then are ye Abraham's seed, and heirs according to the promise."

Deuteronomy 28:1-2 sets out the stipulations of the blessing:

And it shall come to pass, if thou shalt hearken diligently unto the voice of the Lord thy God, to observe and to do all his commandments which I command thee this day, that the Lord thy God will set thee on high above all nations of the earth: And all these blessings shall come on thee, and overtake thee, if thou shalt hearken unto the voice of the Lord thy God.

Then, verses 3-14 list all the blessings of the Law, describing prosperity in every area of life.

Jesus showed how healing is a part of this blessing when He ministered deliverance to a woman in Luke 13:11-13: "And, behold, there was a woman which had a spirit of infirmity eighteen years, and was bowed together, and could in no wise lift up herself. And when Jesus saw her, he called her to him, and said unto her, Woman, thou art loosed from thine infirmity. And he laid his hands on her: and immediately she was made straight, and glorified God."

Because Jesus healed this woman on the Sabbath Day, the ruler of the synagogue was indignant; but Jesus answered him saying: "Thou hypocrite, doth not each one of you on the sabbath loose his ox or his ass from the stall, and lead him away to watering? And ought not this woman, being a daughter of Abraham, whom Satan hath bound, lo, these eighteen years, be loosed from this bond on the sabbath day?" (verses 15-16).

The Abrahamic covenant had been in force for many years. God's people could have walked in health and well-being, but they had become too preoccupied with their religious traditions. The result was a standard of living far below that which God had intended for them.

This woman was a daughter of Abraham and, because of that, she had a right to be loosed from her infirmity. Satan had bound her for 18 years for only one reason: because she was ignorant of her covenant with God. Jesus came and ministered as a prophet under the Abrahamic covenant. He healed the people according to that covenant. He came to set the captives free, and this woman was one of those captives. All she needed was for someone to tell her what was rightfully hers as a daughter of Abraham.

I have good news for you: If that woman could be delivered and set free because she was Abraham's seed, so can you! Because you believe in Jesus Christ and have accepted His sacrifice as your own, you are Abraham's seed and heir to that same promise (Galatians 3:13-14). Praise God, that promise includes physical healing!

Satan has no right to put any sickness, disease or infirmity on your body. You are a child of God, a joint heir with Jesus and a citizen in the kingdom of God. You have a covenant with Almighty God, and one of your covenant rights is the right to a healthy body.

(From: *You Are Healed!* by Kenneth Copeland © 1979 Eagle Mountain International Church Inc. aka Kenneth Copeland Publications)

Evening Reflection

What is a blood covenant?

_____
_____
_____
_____
_____
_____

What blessings were included in God's covenant with Abraham?

_____
_____
_____
_____
_____

What curses did Jesus take on Himself for us?

_____
_____
_____
_____
_____

Notes:

_____
_____
_____
_____
_____
_____
_____
_____
_____
_____
_____
_____
_____
_____
_____
_____

Today's
Prayer of Faith

*Father, thank You that healing is part of salvation for my
spirit, soul and body. You forgave all my sins and healed
all my diseases! I believe You are working in me now.
Thank You for Your Word! In Jesus' Name. Amen.*

_____
_____
_____
_____
_____
_____

REAL-LIFE TESTIMONIES
To Help Build Your Faith

Jesus Did His Part

Five and a half years ago I was diagnosed with stage four ovarian cancer and given no hope of survival. We are so thankful for the teaching we received through KCM and our own pastor.

As soon as surgery was over and we returned home, I ordered Gloria's video *Healing School,* and Dodie Osteen's *Healed of Cancer* book. Due to heavy chemo treatments, I was unable to attend church. KCM became a major ministry to us. We watched it daily. We acted on the Word we heard—we refused to speak words of death and dying.

I've been in and out of treatment over the past five years, and the surgeon says, "You're the greatest miracle I've ever seen in my years of practice." The oncologist doesn't even know what to do anymore; I've gone way beyond his wildest expectations. I now lead two women's Bible studies and co-lead a couples' Bible study with my husband. Probably the most significant thing that happened to me to lift my faith and cause me not to doubt was when I heard Kenneth say, "Jesus already did His part. It is up to us to appropriate what Jesus already did." It even changed my prayer life. I went from *asking* God to heal me, to *thanking* God for what *was* done at Calvary.

L.R.
Michigan

Chapter Four
Healing in Jesus' Ministry

Jesus Healed Them *All*
by Gloria Copeland

"Philip saith unto him, Lord, show us the Father, and it sufficeth us. Jesus saith unto him.... He that hath seen me hath seen the Father.... Believest thou not that I am in the Father, and the Father in me? the words that I speak unto you I speak not of myself: but the Father that dwelleth in me, he doeth the works" (John 14:8-10).

If you want to see the Father, look at Jesus. During His ministry on earth, Jesus revealed to men the express will of God in action. When you have seen Jesus, you have seen the Father.

Jesus did not even speak His own words. He spoke the Father's words. He did not take credit for the works done in His ministry but said that the Father in Him did the works.

Everything He said and did was a picture of the Father's will. Jesus said in John 8:28, *The Amplified Bible*, "I do nothing of Myself (of My own accord or on My own authority), but I say [exactly] what My Father has taught Me." He was God's vehicle on the earth, God's way to man and man's way to God. "For I came down from heaven, not to do mine own will, but the will of him that sent me" (John 6:38). First John 3:8 says, "For this purpose the Son of God was manifested, that he might destroy the works of the devil." Jesus came to do God's will in the earth. His will was for Jesus to destroy the works of the devil. God set Jesus in direct opposition to Satan, the curse and all its evil effects.

Every move Jesus made and every word He said was geared to destroy the work of Satan. Every work of power and every healing was the will of God.

If you believe God's Word, you have to believe that Jesus' attitude toward sickness is God's attitude toward sickness.

He Healed All—Every—Any

Watch God's will concerning healing in the ministry of Jesus. Watch for the words *all, every* and *any.* "But when Jesus knew it, he withdrew himself from thence: and great multitudes followed him, and he healed them *all*" (Matthew 12:15). Even in a great multitude of people, Jesus healed them all. This means that not one was left sick!

"And Jesus went forth, and saw a great multitude, and was moved with compassion toward them, and he healed their sick" (Matthew 14:14). Not just some of their sick—*all* of them.

Matthew 15:30-31 says: "And great multitudes came unto him, having with them those that were lame, blind, dumb, maimed, and many others, and cast them down at Jesus' feet; and he healed them: Insomuch that the multitude wondered, when they saw the dumb to speak, the maimed to be whole, the lame to walk, and the blind to see: and they glorified the God of Israel." (Notice when God gets glory!)

Luke 4:40 says: "Now when the sun was setting, all they that had *any* sick with divers diseases brought them unto him; and he laid his hands on every one of them, and healed them." *Any* who were sick were brought to Him. He laid His hands on *every* one of them and healed them.

Luke 6:17-19 says:

And he came down with them, and stood in the plain, and the company of his disciples, and a great multitude of people out of all Judaea and Jerusalem, and from the sea coast of Tyre and Sidon, which came to hear him, and to be healed of their diseases; and they that were vexed with unclean spirits: and they were healed. And the whole multitude sought to touch him: for there went virtue out of him, and healed them *all*.

The multitude came to hear Jesus, but they also came to be healed. They came expecting to receive. They knew that if they could get where Jesus was, they would receive healing. They came to be healed! He healed them *all*. Not even in a great multitude was there a person that Jesus would not heal. You know that in a great multitude there were all kinds of people—good and bad, but Jesus healed them all. If there was anything that could disqualify one from receiving healing, surely in a great multitude you would find one who was so bad that he could not receive. And yet, *Jesus healed them all!* Thank God the Bible tells us in Hebrews 13:8 that He is the same yesterday, today and forever.

We have a covenant with God, and Jesus has already paid the price for our sicknesses and diseases. Every one of us should be loosed from the bondage of Satan. We have the same authority to do just what Jesus did—to command sickness and disease to depart. Remember the woman in Luke 13 whom Ken talked about in the last session? She was a daughter of Abraham who had to be reminded of her covenant rights. Jesus said, "Woman, thou art loosed from thine infirmity" and she was made straight.

Jesus executed judgment in that situation, and she was loosed from the bondage of Satan. This is a picture of the Church executing judgment in the earth. When you lay hands on the sick, you are executing judgment—declaring that the prince of this world (Satan) has been judged and that the power of sickness and disease has been destroyed (John 16:11). The authority in the Name of Jesus belongs to you because you are a believer. In His Name you are taking authority over sickness and disease in another person's body and commanding it to leave. It will go! The Word says if you resist the devil, he will flee from you (James 4:7). As God's representative, you can cast out devils. You can lay hands on the sick, and they will recover.

Let Go of Doubt

Look at Acts 10:38 and see how Peter describes Jesus' ministry after three years of close association with Him: "How God anointed Jesus of Nazareth with the Holy Ghost and with power: who went about doing good, and healing all that were oppressed of the devil; for God was with him." Did He just heal some? No. He healed *all* who were oppressed of the devil.

The only record of anything hindering Jesus from accomplishing the will of God in the lives of His people occurred in Nazareth. It was not God's will that stopped His miracle and healing power; it was the will of the people there. He could do no mighty works because of their unbelief (Mark 6:5-6). Doubt will rob you of God's blessings. Unbelief will rob you and leave you sick. There is only one thing that can stop doubt and unbelief in the heart of a man and that is the Word of God. When a person receives the Word, doubt, defeat and discouragement have to leave. Don't

hang on to any doubt or unbelief. Don't even dwell on it. Let the Word of God expel it.

I absolutely refuse to feed my spirit on doubt and unbelief because I know that my very life depends on the faith of God in my spirit. I will not sit under any teacher or preacher who puts doubt and unbelief in my spirit. What you feed into your spirit is a matter of life and death, of victory and defeat. Faith comes by hearing the Word of God. Doubt comes by hearing unbelief. It is important what you hear.

Scripture shows beyond doubt that Jesus, while fulfilling the will of God, offered healing unconditionally during His ministry in the earth. God has never been stingy with His healing power. He has always desired that you be healed. He wants you to be healed even more than you do. Because of His great compassion and love for His family, God greatly desires to manifest His power in our midst, yet He works only by faith—no other way.

(From: *And Jesus Healed Them All* by Gloria Copeland © 1981 International Church of the Word of Faith Inc. now known as Eagle Mountain International Church aka Kenneth Copeland Publications)

How does Jesus reveal God's attitude toward sickness?

_____

_____

_____

_____

_____

Jesus healed _all_ who came to Him during His earthly ministry. How do we know He's willing to do the same today?

_____

_____

_____

_____

_____

How can you combat doubt and unbelief?

_____

_____

_____

_____

_____

Today's
Connection Points

- **_Healing Praise_ CD: "Jesus Healed Them All" (Track 2)**

  Jesus healed them _all,_ and that includes _you._ Focus on that truth with today's selection.

- **_Healing Scriptures_ CD: Track 3**

  Feed your spirit over and over with these powerful scriptures that prove God's will is for you to be healed.

  Matthew 12:9-13, 22, 14:14, 34-36, 15:30-31, 20:30-34, 21:14; Mark 1:40-42

- **DVD: "Health to Your Body" (Chapter 4)**

  We are not like those without hope! Watch as Gloria teaches how departing from disobedience is health for your whole body.

 As you read the Word, see the Father's heart in the life of Jesus.

Let faith remove any doubt and unbelief.

Notes:

_____

_____

_____

_____

_____

_____

_____

_____

_____

_____

_____

_____

_____

_____

_____

_____

_____

_____

Healing Always Comes

by Kenneth Copeland

Your days of sickness and disease are over. I'll never forget the day God spoke those words to me. It was some of the best news I'd ever heard. I believed it and have been walking in the glorious truth of it for decades now.

If you're sitting there right now, wishing God would say those same words to you, I have good news for you: He has.

He has said it to every one of us.

He said it with such power and force that it made hell tremble and heaven ring. He wrote it in the covenant blood of His own Son. He shouted it down through the ages through prophets and apostles and preachers.

The problem is, most Christians haven't truly heard it. They haven't let it reach down into their hearts and become truth to them. God has said it...but they haven't yet believed.

If that is the case with you today, I want you to know that this one truth I'm about to share with you will forever alter how you understand God's willingness to heal. It will put to rest every doubt about God's will for your healing and open the door of divine health to you.

Stories and Lies

Of course, some sincere-hearted believers have gotten confused about healing because they've seen or heard of instances where a good Christian didn't receive it. We've all heard the stories. "Well, healing couldn't be included in redemption because Sister So-and-So who taught Sunday school every week for 65 years got sick and God didn't heal her."

I want you to know something about those stories: They are lies. Granted, those who tell them usually don't realize it, but they are lies just the same.

I realize that's a shockingly blunt statement, but the Bible itself is just that blunt. It says: "What if some did not believe and were without faith? Does their lack of faith and their faithlessness nullify and make ineffective and void the faithfulness of God and His fidelity [to His Word]? By no means! Let God be found true though every human being is false and a liar" (Romans 3:3-4, *The Amplified Bible*).

God has made His Word plain to us. He has said, "With his stripes we are healed" (Isaiah 53:5). He has said, "The prayer of faith shall save the sick, and the Lord shall raise him up" (James 5:15). He has said, "[Jesus] Himself took our infirmities, and bare our sicknesses" (Matthew 8:17).

God always keeps His Word. Here's

what I want you to understand: *Healing always comes*.

Healing always comes! The problem has been in our receiving, not in God's giving.

Put that over in the realm of the new birth and you can easily see what I mean. The Bible says that by the righteousness of one, the free gift has come upon all men (Romans 5:18). Jesus has already gone to the cross and been raised from the dead. He has reconciled us to God and made righteousness available to every person on the face of the earth.

Therefore, it always comes. To whom? To anyone who will obey the instructions in Romans 10:9-10: "If thou shalt confess with thy mouth the Lord Jesus, and shalt believe in thine heart that God hath raised him from the dead, thou shalt be saved. For with the heart man believeth unto righteousness; and with the mouth confession is made unto salvation."

Healing comes to the same people. It comes to those who will believe in their hearts that Jesus was crucified and raised from the dead to purchase their healing. It comes to those who will open their mouths in faith and say, "Glory to God, I receive it. I am healed!"

Make an Effort

When the enemy comes at you with symptoms of sickness, you won't crawl up in the bed and whine, "Why does this always happen to me?" You'll stomp your foot and say, "Glory be to God, this body is off limits to you, Satan. I refuse to allow you to put that foul thing on my body after Jesus has already borne it for me. So you might as well pack it up and go home right now!"

I'm not saying it will be easy. It won't be. Not in this life. Not in this world. Just as you don't live in victory over sin without putting forth an effort, you can't bumble along in life and have God just drop healing in your lap.

No, you'll have to stand for it. You'll have to fight the good fight of faith.

But don't let that scare you. It's a fight you can win. I know you can because 2,000 years ago, Jesus gave you everything you'd ever need to win it. He took your weakness and gave you His strength. He took your sin and gave you His righteousness. He took your sickness and gave you His health. He took your every defeat and gave you His victory in its place.

You are the heir of the Greatest Exchange ever made.

(From: *One Word From God Can Change Your Health* by Kenneth and Gloria Copeland © 1999 Kenneth and Gloria Copeland)

Evening Reflection

How does healing come to the believer?

_____
_____
_____
_____
_____

How often does healing come to the believer?

_____
_____
_____
_____
_____

Why must we make an effort to receive healing?

_____
_____
_____
_____
_____
_____
_____

Notes:

_____
_____
_____
_____
_____
_____
_____
_____
_____
_____

Today's Prayer of Faith

*Thank You, Lord, for taking my sin and sickness on the
cross. Nothing can change that. You have already healed
all my sickness and disease. I believe I receive it now.
Your living Word is powerful and working in me. In Jesus'
Name. Amen. Healed and Praising God*

REAL-LIFE TESTIMONIES
To Help Build Your Faith

Healed and Praising God

I had a stomachache and had made my healing confessions, prayed with
friends and also been to hospital—scans were made and tests were done,
but the doctors found nothing. I kept standing on 1 Peter 2:24.

One evening last week on the *BVOV* broadcast, Gloria prayed and
made some declarations. She said we should get up and do whatever
we couldn't do before. Because of the stomachache, I couldn't walk
too well, but thanks to the healing power in Jesus Christ, I was able to
walk and started running about. The pain was gone! Thank God for the
effectiveness of the Word and for using Gloria to pray and believe God
with me. I am also growing day by day in my faith, prayer life, love walk
and my personal relationship with God and the Holy Spirit through the
teachings of Kenneth and Gloria Copeland.

A.K.
United Kingdom

Chapter Five
Planting God's Word in Your Heart

God's Prescription
by Gloria Copeland

"My son, attend to my words; incline thine ear unto my sayings. Let them not depart from thine eyes; keep them in the midst of thine heart. For they are life unto those that find them, and health to all their flesh. Keep thy heart with all diligence; for out of it are the issues of life" (Proverbs 4:20-23).

These verses describe God's prescription for life and health. If you are well, God's Word will keep you well. If you are sick, it will heal you and then keep you well. There has never been a miracle drug that could equal the Word of God. God's medicine is the answer to every need.

Let's break down these verses and really look at what God is telling us.

"Attend to My Words"

This means you must give your undivided attention to God's Word. Pay heed to what He says. Whatever it says, you believe it and act on it. If you attend to someone, you take care of that person. The Word of God is the one thing that a believer cannot successfully do without. If you will attend to the Word and spend time in it, every other situation in your life will be taken care of because of the faith, knowledge and

wisdom that come from God's Word. Everything we do should revolve around the Word of God because it has the answer to every problem. The Word of God will make your time count. It will save you from making mistakes that cost time. Sickness costs time. The Word of God will make your life better and your time more productive. You cannot afford to be without the Word.

Whenever I get under pressure and begin to think, *There's no way that I can do all I've got to do,* I know immediately that I have not been spending enough time in God's Word. When I get bogged down in the affairs of life and pressure comes, I know that my time in the Word has gone for something else. The Word of God causes your life to *work.* You won't get bogged down in the affairs of life if you will spend time in the Word, meditate in it and see what God is saying to you.

The Bible says, "Thou wilt keep him in perfect peace, whose mind is stayed on thee: because he trusteth in thee" (Isaiah 26:3). When you spend time in the Word and stay your mind on it, you will be kept in perfect peace and you will trust in Him. That is faith. Romans 10:17 says faith comes by hearing and hearing by the Word of God. You will be kept in this perfect peace because you trust in Him. Your faith will stay strong and you will be trusting in the Lord, not in the things you can see.

When you keep your attention on God's Word, your mind will be free from doubt. Many people try to believe, but don't have the Word in their hearts. Faith is not a mental process. Believing in the heart comes from time spent in the Word of God. It takes more than just a mental decision to cause your vocabulary to be in line with God's Word.

Jesus said, "Out of the abundance of the heart the mouth speaketh" (Matthew 12:34). You have to get God's Word into your heart in abundance so that it has more reality to you than the things you see. In other words, if you're sick, you need to come to a place where the Word of God has so much reality to you that the symptoms in your body count for nothing. That's what Abraham did. He was fully persuaded that God was able and mighty to keep His Word (Romans 4:21). It didn't matter to him that he was 100 years old and that the time for Sarah to bear children had passed. He didn't look at that. He was fully persuaded that the Word of God was true.

You have to put the Word of God in your heart until the reality of your healing has more power and validity to you than the symptoms of sickness coming on your body. That revelation will only come from attending to God's Word—keeping yourself in the Word of God and putting it in your heart in abundance. You can come to the place where the Word of God has more authority than what you can see or feel. If you see or feel something that is oppo-site from the Word, you'll not be moved by it because you are moved only by God's Word.

"Incline Thine Ear Unto My Sayings"

We must desire and go after God's Word. Put your ear in position to hear the word of faith preached. Don't wait for someone to come to your town. Go to where the Word is being preached. Believers are moving from one city to another because they want to get under the Word and receive what God has for them. They are going to any lengths to get under the Word. They know that if they get the Word in their hearts, they can get anything else they need. If you spend enough time in the Word, it will change everything you do.

Jesus said: "If any man has ears to hear, let him be listening and let him perceive and comprehend. And He said to them, Be careful what you are hearing. The measure [of thought and study] you give [to the truth you hear] will be the measure [of virtue and knowledge] that comes back to you—and more [besides] will be given to you who hear (Mark 4:23-24, *The Amplified Bible*).

We measure to ourselves the blessing of the Lord by the attention, respect and heed we give to His Word. If you give just a little heed to it, that's all you are going to receive. If you give total heed and attention to God's Word, the power that comes back to you will be great, and it will produce results in your life.

Jesus said to be careful how you hear. Remember: Don't hear through tradition. Don't make the Word of God sift its way through traditional ears. It won't work for you. Receive God's Word willingly. Allow it to be unhindered by anything you have ever known or experienced.

To prosper in the faith walk, you must first make a decision that God's Word does not fail. If the Word of God does not seem to be working for you, it's not God's fault. There is something you don't know. More than likely, you are just not standing firm. The Bible says, "And having done all, to stand. Stand therefore..." (Ephesians 6:13-14). It says, "Stand." That's all. It doesn't say for how long. If you catch yourself saying, "Well, the Word is not working for me," then you can know automatically that you are not standing. You must have a steadfast faith when it comes to God's Word. If it is not steadfast, it is not faith. One thing you must know is: *God's Word does not fail!*

These things work for the obedient. When God said, "I am the Lord that healeth thee," He said that they were to serve Him. When He said, "I will take sickness away from the midst of thee," He also said, "if you will serve Me." In other places He says, "If you are diligent to do My Word...." There are things we can do in order to be in line with the healing power of God. Make the decision to know that failure is not on God's part. It is not a failure of His Word. God doesn't make mistakes, but His children do. When Satan tries to make you mad at God and you say, "God, I've done all these things. I've confessed Your Word and it's not working for me," you can remember that it is not God. God never fails. The Word never fails. Don't test and examine God. Test and examine yourself. Don't judge God. Judge yourself.

"Let Them Not Depart From Thine Eyes"

Keep your eyes trained on the Word of God. Don't look at the circumstances that appear contrary to what you are believing for. Keep your eyes on the Word of God. Be like Abraham and consider the Word instead of your body. What you receive through your eyes and ears can make the difference between life and death, so keep the Word before your eyes and going in your ears. What you believe in your heart is regulated by what you give your attention to.

"Keep Them in the Midst of Thine Heart"

Keep the Word of God alive in your heart. Keep it working in your heart. Just as you feed your physical man, you must feed your spiritual man. Your spirit man cannot live and stay strong on the Word you received last year. Don't try to rely on what you remember from the Word. Keep God's words in the midst of your heart by doing the things we have already discussed: Attend to the Word, incline your ear to the Word, don't let the Word depart from your eyes, and keep the Word in your heart. Keep your spirit strong with the Word of God. Continually feed yourself with it in order to keep the Word producing the force of faith.

"For They Are Life Unto Those That Find Them and Health to All Their Flesh"

God's words are spirit and they are life (John 6:63). They are made life and health to those who find them. The Word of God is medicine. If you will put it in your heart in abundance, it will be as hard for you to get sick as it was at one time for you to get healed. (The key to this statement is in the word *abundance!*) God's prescription for life and health works constantly, whether you are sick or well. The Word is continually being made life and health to your body. Satan cannot make you sick when you stay strong in the Word and keep your spirit full of God's Word. By keeping the Word in the midst of your heart, the healing power of God will continually work in your body. It is continually being made health to your flesh.

When the doctor prescribes medication, he tells you to take the medicine a certain number of times a day and you will recover. If you expect to be well, you follow his instructions, don't you? Well, this is *God's* prescription. His Word is His medicine. If you will do what He says as diligently as you would obey a doctor, you will get results.

Diligence in the Word of God is key. When your doctor says you need surgery, you don't say, "Well, Doc, I don't have time to have an operation." No, you make time, even if you lose your job. Be that courageous, diligent and determined about the Word of God. Make time to attend to God's Word. It will bring far better results!

"Keep Thy Heart With All Diligence"

Be diligent about keeping God's Word in your heart. Continually attending to it with your ears, your eyes and your heart will cause you to live in divine health. The Word of God will continually be made life and health to your body. Don't attend to the sickness. Attend to God's Word. Whether you are sick or well, the Word is continually made life and health to your flesh. This is the surest way to stay healed. To be sick and then receive healing is not God's best. God's best is for you to live in divine health, to have divine life continually flowing from your spirit man to your physical man—keeping your physical body well. "But if the Spirit of him that raised up Jesus from the dead dwell in you, he that raised up Christ from the dead shall also quicken your mortal bodies by his Spirit that dwelleth in you" (Romans 8:11).

"For Out of It Are the Issues of Life"

The forces of life bring healing power. Out of your heart comes the force of faith to relieve you of any problem that Satan would try to bring on you. God's best is for you to keep your heart with all diligence and have the forces of life continually coming out of your spirit. This realm of God's very best is available to every one of us if we will spend time in the Word. The forces of life and power coming from the heart are in direct proportion to the amount of Word going in us and the attention or heed we give it. There is no limit to the amount of God's medicine you can take. You cannot overdose. The more you take, the stronger you get.

(From: *And Jesus Healed Them All* by Gloria Copeland © 1981 International Church of the Word of Faith Inc. now known as Eagle Mountain International Church aka Kenneth Copeland Publications)

Briefly describe God's prescription for divine health.

_____

_____

_____

_____

_____

_____

_____

_____

_____

What should you do if you're feeding yourself with the Word but not yet seeing results?

_____

_____

_____

_____

_____

_____

_____

_____

_____

How does putting God's Word in your heart turn into health for your body?

_____

_____

_____

_____

_____

_____

_____

Today's  Connection Points

- ### *Healing Praise* CD: "More Precious Than Silver"/ "O Come Let Us Adore Him" (Medley) (Track 8)

  As you give the Word of God top priority in your life, let the words of these songs express your heart.

- ### *Healing Scriptures* CD: Tracks 4-6

  Give your attention to God's Word as you listen to these healing scriptures.

  > Mark 5:21-43, 6:12-13, 53-56, 7:32-37, 8:22-25, 16:17-18; Luke 4:16-18, 5:15, 17, 6:17-19, 7:11-16, 9:1-2, 13:10-17; John 5:1-3, 5-9

- ### DVD: "With His Stripes" (Chapter 5)

  Enjoy another inspiring testimony today and listen to great teaching on how easy it is to receive from Jesus…because of His sacrifice for us.

Faith  in Action

 ## Be diligent to study God's Word.
Allow its truths to become more real to you than circumstances.

Notes:

_____

_____

_____

_____

_____

_____

_____

The Last Word
by Kenneth Copeland

Do you feel caught in a spiritual stalemate? You pray, fast and shout the Name of Jesus a hundred times—but your healing doesn't seem any closer at all.

Let me tell you from experience, when that happens, it's time to ask yourself a crucial question. It's one you should have asked from the get-go—and it's the only question that will get you out. "What does the Word of God have to say about this?"

Jesus called Himself the Alpha and Omega, the First and the Last (Revelation 1:11). His Word carries absolute and final authority in every area and on every topic.

I don't know why Christian people allow themselves to slip into a habit of praying about things without paying any attention to what the Bible has to say about them, but they do. The Word should be our very foundation on such matters.

Many times even our prayers themselves go crosswise to the Word. Have you ever heard anyone pray, "If it be Thy will, heal me"? But if that person had been in the Word, he would have realized that God revealed His will once and for all when He laid our sicknesses on Jesus. Giving us that revelation cost Him dearly. Once, when He spoke to me of Calvary, He said, *It is as close to Me as if it had happened today. It is burned into My consciousness.*

How dare we, then, ignore the Word and tell some sick brother that it is God's will for him to be sick a little longer so he can learn something?

Isaiah 53:10 says, "It was the will of the Lord to bruise Him; He has put Him to grief and made Him sick" *(The Amplified Bible)*. If it was the will of God to bruise Jesus and make Him carry our sicknesses, how can it be the will of God to bruise us and make us carry those same sicknesses again? It can't be! That would be a travesty of divine justice!

If we want to pray powerful prayers—prayers that are heard in heaven and shake the earth—we must start with the Word of God. I'm going to say it again. If we'd learn to start our prayers, our fasting and everything else on the Word, we'd begin seeing results!

The Power of Consistency

There's a word in the Bible you see all the time. You can find it in Colossians. It's the word *continue*. It smacks of discipline. Continue in the faith. Continue in the Word. Continue in prayer. Be constant in season and out. That's Bible talk.

There's a revelation of God that comes from consistency that the inconsistent person will never see, and that revelation will bring you the kind of continual health and success you've always dreamed of.

Let me illustrate what I mean. Say, for example, there are two men, both building a house. You ask one what he's doing and he says, "I'm building a house." You ask the other and he says, "I'm serving God."

Now when the guy who's just building a house gets in trouble (and he'll get into trouble with almost every house he builds), he'll run to God.

But the other guy who's serving God by building this house won't have to go through that trouble. That's because he talks to God about everything as he goes along. He hardly even hammers a nail without talking it over with God. If it's necessary, God may wake that brother up in the middle of the night and say, *Listen, you have that foundation started wrong. You need to go back and change it.*

Now why wouldn't God do that same thing for the first guy? He loves them both, so why would He help only one? Because the other guy wouldn't wake up in the night. He couldn't hear God's voice. He wasn't in the habit of listening.

If you're not walking in the Word consistently, you won't hear God. The reason is simple. Have you ever called someone on the telephone and they didn't recognize your voice? Why didn't they? They hadn't heard it enough. If you don't "continue," as the Bible says, in your communications with God,

that's what will happen when He tries to speak to you. You won't recognize His voice.

So start bringing Him in at the beginning. Make His Word the Alpha word, the place you begin. It will keep you in divine health so you never get sick in the first place. There are thousands of promises in the Bible, and they all belong to you. Dig in and find out for yourself, what they say.

You won't ever discover the real power in prayer until you begin to base your praying on the Word. When I started doing that, taking the Word personally and acting on it, my experience of it changed. It began to talk to me. It began to be the answer to my prayer.

Suddenly I understood what God meant when He said His Word wouldn't return to Him void (Isaiah 55:11). I'd wondered about that for years. I didn't know if God's Word was supposed to bounce off the earth and back up to heaven or what. But I began to see that when I started putting His Word in my prayers and sending it back to Him in faith, things started changing in my life. My prayers started accomplishing something.

Colossians 3:17 says, "Whatsoever ye do in word or deed, do all in the name of the Lord Jesus." Every word and every deed, do it in Jesus' Name. Well, how are you going to do anything in the Name of Jesus without knowing what Jesus said about it? You can't speak in the name of the law or anyone else without knowing what you're representing. If you speak in their name, you're speaking according to their word, so you'd better know what they said!

When I speak in Jesus' Name about my health, for example, I go by what He says about it. He says He bore all my sins in His own body on the tree (1 Peter 2:24). He says by His stripes I was healed. That's not even a promise. It's a fact.

Once I discovered that, I made it part of my vocabulary. If someone asks me, "How are you?" I answer according to what Jesus said. I don't answer based on the feelings of my body. That's changeable. His Word never changes.

If you tell me, "Boy, you sure don't look healed," I just smile. If you're moved by how I look, I'm just glad you're not the one I'm praying to. I never talk to God about how I look. He's not moved by that. I just talk to Him about His Word. That's what Colossians means when it says, "Continue in the faith grounded and settled, and be not moved away from the hope of the gospel." You can't be moved. You must have your faith grounded in the Word.

Got Faith?

As a young Christian, I found out that the one with the faith is the one with the power. I made up my mind to be a man of power, so I set out to "get faith."

I went to church Sunday after Sunday, trying to find out where I could get it, but no one helped me. They told me how important it was to have faith and what great things would happen if you had it, but I never could figure out where I was supposed to get it.

Finally, I started getting into the Word of God. I came across scriptures like Romans 10:8-9, 17—it revolutionized my whole life! "The word is nigh thee," it said, "even in thy mouth, and in thy heart: that is, the word of faith, which we preach; that if thou shalt confess with thy mouth the Lord Jesus, and shalt believe in thine heart that God hath raised him from the dead, thou shalt be saved.... So then faith cometh by hearing, and hearing by the word of God."

How does faith come? *By hearing the Word of God.* Anyone who's believed that Jesus is the Son of God and confessed Him with their mouth as their Lord, has had the faith of God imparted into their spirit. It's already in there. You don't have to pray for it. It's there, and when you put the Word of God in there, that faith will come forth.

Jesus always talked about faith as if it were alive. He called it a seed. When His disciples asked Him how to get more of it, He said, plant it and it will grow. You don't make the seed big and then plant it. You plant the seed and it grows big.

How do you plant it? You start with the Word. Remember what Jesus said, "The sower soweth the *word.*" When you're ready to grow some faith, you plant the Word in your heart. You study it. You meditate on it. You settle it in your heart. It becomes your Alpha word, the word you're beginning on. Faith rises up on the inside of you because faith comes by hearing the Word of God.

What do you do then? You act on the Word. That's how faith is released. You speak to the mountain. Tell the problem what the Word says about it. You tell it, in Jesus' Name, that it's going to have to move.

Did you know that what you say is very, very important? Jesus' half brother James said if you control your tongue, you control your whole body. He said the tongue is like kindling to a fire. Everything that happens in your life begins with it. So you can imagine what kind of power is generated in your life when you choose to speak God's Word and His Spirit is behind what you say.

Jesus spoke to the wind and to the sea. He spoke to the fig tree; and every time He spoke, whatever He said happened. Do you know why? He tells you in John 12:49. There He says: *I don't speak My own words. I say what My Father tells Me to say.*

Jesus spoke God's words. When we learn to speak what God says instead of what everyone else is saying, we're going to see the same results Jesus saw. We're not just going to see them every once in a while either, we're going to see them consistently.

Start going to Jesus for the first word in every situation. Take time. I don't care how long it takes you to search it out and find what His promises are that cover that situation. You don't have anything more important to do than that. It's your Alpha word. It's where your victory begins. And it will get you out of any spiritual stalemate.

(From: the *Believer's Voice of Victory* magazine, September 1990)

Evening Reflection

Why is consistency so important when studying the Word?

_____

_____

_____

_____

How does faith come?

_____

_____

_____

_____

How do you release faith?

_____

_____

_____

_____

Notes:

_____
_____
_____
_____
_____
_____
_____
_____
_____
_____
_____
_____
_____
_____
_____
_____

Today's
Prayer of Faith

Father, as I study and meditate on Your Word, I am convinced in my heart that You want me to live in health. I know it is Your will. I thank You for working in me as I decide to walk in health, and take action every day. In Jesus' Name. Amen.

_____
_____
_____
_____
_____
_____
_____
_____

REAL-LIFE TESTIMONIES
To Help Build Your Faith

"This Baby Shall Live!"

In August 2006, my daughter, who was about 20 weeks pregnant, began to miscarry. The doctor prepared her for the worst. Meanwhile at home, my husband and I began to stand on God's Word that our children are blessed. I recalled Kenneth and Gloria's story about their granddaughter being stricken with meningitis and how they came together and took Communion over the situation. We took Communion and told the devil he had no authority—that the blood of Jesus is over our descendants.

My daughter later had an ultrasound, which showed a blood clot had formed between the uterine wall and placenta, separating the two. The doctor's report was that there was no way life could carry on. My daughter and her husband stood on the Word that their unborn child "shall not die but live and declare the works of God."

A week later a specialist performed another ultrasound and found that although there was a blood clot, everything else was normal. On Jan. 26, 2007, a healthy baby boy was born! To God be the glory!

D.H.
Michigan

Chapter Six
Speaking the Word

What Did You Say?
by Gloria Copeland

What happens when your heart gets so full it starts to overflow? Look at Matthew 12:34 and you'll see. It says, "...out of the abundance of the heart the mouth speaketh."

The last step of God's divine prescription is to speak, not words of sickness and disease, discouragement and despair, but words of healing and life, faith and hope. You are to: "Put away from thee a froward mouth, and perverse lips put far from thee" (Proverbs 4:24). In short, you are to speak the words of God.

Initially, that may not be easy for you to do. If you're like most people, you've probably spent years talking about how bad things are. At the first sniffle or sneeze, you may be likely to say, "I must be catching a cold. I get one every year!" You may not even mean it. But you've spoken like that for so long, it's become habit.

What's more, people are comfortable with that kind of talk. They'll jump right in and say, "Yeah, the same thing happens to me." But when you start speaking the Word, you'll sneeze and say, "I resist you, cold! I call myself healed, in Jesus' Name! I believe I'm taking healing!"

That will sound so different to other people. That's OK. Talk the Word anyway because for faith to work it must be in two places—in your heart and in your mouth. "For with the heart man believeth unto righteousness; and with the mouth confession is made unto salvation" (Romans 10:10).

Some people say that faith will move mountains. But, the scriptural truth is, faith won't even move a molehill for you unless you release it with the words of your mouth.

The Lord Jesus told us that "whosoever shall *say* unto this mountain, Be thou removed, and be thou cast into the sea; and shall not doubt in his heart, but shall believe that those things which he *saith* shall come to pass; he shall have whatsoever he *saith*" (Mark 11:23). Notice the word *say* appears three times in that verse while the word *believe* appears only once. Obviously, Jesus wanted us to know that our words are crucial.

It's also important to note that He did not instruct us to talk *about* the mountain, but to talk *to* it! If we're going to obey Him, we must talk to the mountain of sickness and cast it out of our lives. The Lord told Charles Capps, *I have told My people they can have what they say, but they are saying what they have!* Instead of saying, "I'm healed," most Christians say, "I'm sick" and reinforce the sickness or disease.

I know one minister who went to visit a young man in the hospital years ago. The fellow was unconscious and had been given up to die by the doctors. As the minister was leaving the hospital room, the Lord spoke to him to let the young man's wife know that her husband would be healed if she would obey Mark 11:23.

So, she did! Day after day, she sat next to her unconscious husband and said, "My husband will live and not die, in Jesus' Name...My husband will live and not die, in Jesus' Name." As a result, that young man was fully healed.

No Time Like the Present

Of course, don't wait until you have a need to start speaking the Word. Start speaking it now.

I'll never forget the first time I realized the importance of speaking God's Word. It was years ago when Ken had just started preaching, and I was staying at home with our children. We were in a desperate situation financially, and I was eager for answers.

One day as I was sitting at my typewriter, listening to tapes and typing notes, I read Mark 11:23 and the last phrase jumped out at me: "he shall have whatsoever he saith." The Lord spoke to my heart and said, *In consistency lies the power.*

He was telling me that it's not just the words you speak when you pray that change things, it's the words you speak *all* the time!

If you want to see your desire come to pass, you need to make your words match your prayers. Don't try to pray in faith and then get up and talk in unbelief. Talk faith all the time!

Romans 4:17 says God "...calleth those things which be not as though they were." So if you want to receive something from God, follow His example. Speak it. That's the way faith works. You speak the Word of God concerning what you want to happen.

If what you're looking for is health, then go to the Word that tells you, "By His stripes you were healed," and put that in your mouth. Don't talk sickness. Talk health. Don't talk the problem. Talk the answer.

Be Like Abraham

"But, Gloria, it bothers me to say I'm healed when my body still feels sick!"

It shouldn't. It didn't bother Abraham. He went around calling himself the father of nations for years even though he was as childless as could be. Why did he do it? Because "he believed...God, who quickeneth the dead, and calleth those things which be not as though they were" (Romans 4:17). He was "fully persuaded that, what [God] had promised, he was able also to perform" (verse 21).

You see, Abraham wasn't "trying" to believe God. He wasn't just mentally assenting to it. He had immersed himself in God's Word until that Word was more real to him than the things he could see. It didn't matter to him that he was 100 years old. It didn't matter to him that Sarah was far past the age of childbearing and that she had been barren all her life. All that mattered to him was what God said because he knew His Word was true.

If you don't have that kind of faith for healing right now, then stay in the Word until you get it! After all, "faith cometh by hearing, and hearing by the word of God" (Romans 10:17). Read, study, meditate, listen to audio resources and watch videos of good, faith-filled teaching. Go through this study again and again, watch our Sunday and daily television broadcast *every day* until God's Word about healing is more real to you than the symptoms in your body. Keep on keeping on until, like Abraham, you stagger not at the promise of God through unbelief, but grow strong in faith as you give praise and glory to God. (See Romans 4:20, *The Amplified Bible.*)

Notice that last phrase doesn't say you give praise to God *because* you're strong in faith. It says you grow strong in faith *as* you give praise to Him. I like that particular translation because I've found it to be true. Praising God for your healing is one of the most powerful things you can do.

In fact, Psalm 103 *commands* us to do it. It says, "Bless the Lord, O my soul: and all that is within me, bless his holy name. Bless the Lord, O my soul, and forget not all his benefits: who forgiveth all thine iniquities; who healeth all thy diseases" (verses 1-3).

So start speaking the Word of God today. Call things which be not as though they were. As you do, your faith will strengthen and your healing will come!

(From: *Harvest of Health* by Gloria Copeland © 1992 Eagle Mountain International Church Inc. aka Kenneth Copeland Ministries and *God's Prescription for Divine Health* by Gloria Copeland © 1995 Eagle Mountain International Church Inc. aka Kenneth Copeland Ministries)

Morning Reflection

Why is it important to speak God's Word concerning your health?

_____
_____
_____
_____
_____
_____
_____
_____
_____
_____
_____

According to Romans 4:17, what things in your life "which be not" are you going to call "as though they were"?

_____
_____
_____
_____
_____
_____
_____
_____
_____
_____
_____
_____
_____
_____

How is it truthful to say you're healed when your body still feels sick?

_____
_____
_____
_____
_____
_____
_____
_____
_____
_____
_____
_____

Today's Connection Points

- ⊙ *Healing Praise* **CD: "All-Consuming Fire" (Track 10)**

  The Lord is our all-consuming fire! Praise Him with this song as you speak His Word aloud.

- ⊙ *Healing Scriptures* **CD: Track 8**

  Feed your spirit with healing scriptures that prove your healing takes place when you pray!

    Mark 11:24; Acts 3:2-9, 5:16

- ⊙ **DVD: "Curing Them All" (Chapter 6)**

  Strengthen your faith with more teaching on how Jesus healed them all...and that means you!

Faith in Action

 Make it standard practice to speak God's Word instead of unbelief.
Start living differently!

Notes:

_____

_____

_____

_____

_____

_____

_____

Evening Connection

The Power of Words
by Kenneth Copeland

"**D**eath and life are in the power of the tongue, and they who indulge in it shall eat the fruit of it [for death or life]" (Proverbs 18:21, *The Amplified Bible*).

There is a Bible secret about words. Words are spiritual. They carry power. James' epistle to the Church has a message that is vital to our understanding of the power of words. Before we go any further, I want you to get your Bible and read the entire third chapter of James very closely. And remember, James was the brother of Jesus. He saw Jesus in day-to-day situations his whole life. He knew what he was talking about, and it's interesting that he focuses so strongly on the power of words.

The Tongue—Small, But Big!

Having read James 3, you'll notice there are two central ideas:

1. There is nothing in this earth so great, so powerful, including the physical body, that cannot be controlled by the tongue.
2. The entire course of nature and the circumstances sur-

rounding every human being are controlled by that person's tongue.

Your tongue is the deciding factor in your life. No matter how fierce the storm or how serious the problem, your tongue will turn it. Your confession will control your ship in the storm.

Remember, death and life are in the power of the tongue, and they that indulge it will eat the fruit of it. The fruit of your mouth—whether good or evil, a blessing or a curse—will manifest itself in your life. Jesus said it is not what goes into a man that defiles him, it's what comes out his mouth (Matthew 15:11-18).

Most of us have been trained since birth to speak negative, death-dealing words. Unconsciously, in your everyday conversation, you probably use words of death, sickness, lack, fear, doubt and unbelief: That scared me to death. That tickled me to death. I laughed until I thought I would die. I'm just dying to go. That makes me sick. I'm sick and tired of this mess. I believe I'm getting the flu. We just can't afford it. I doubt it.

You say these things without even realizing it. When you do, you set in motion negative forces in your life and the fire blazes. Now you can understand why James 3:10 says, "Out of the same mouth proceedeth blessing and cursing."

Speaking the Word in Faith

So how do you make a change? Get the Word of God down deep into your spirit man. Jesus said, "Out of the abundance of the heart the mouth speaketh" (Matthew 12:34). When the Word is in your heart in abundance, it will come out of your mouth. By speaking God's Word, you replace the negative forces at work in your life with the positive forces from the good treasures of your heart.

Just as your words loosed the power of Satan, your words loose the power of God. Your words brought death and sickness, but God's Word in your mouth will bring life and healing. Your words produced poverty and lack, but God's Word will produce prosperity and abundance.

The spiritual principle of Mark 11:23 is basic to your life as a born-again believer. That is how God uses His faith. Jesus Himself said, "Have faith in God" (verse 22), or as the cross-reference says, "Have the faith of God." Then He continued to explain how the faith of God works. Notice the close connection between confessing with the mouth and believing with the heart: "Whosoever shall say unto this mountain, Be thou removed, and be thou cast into the sea; and shall not doubt in his heart, but shall believe that those things which he saith shall come to pass; he shall have whatsoever he saith."

Your own salvation was based on words. Romans 10:9-10 says, "If thou shalt confess with thy mouth the Lord Jesus, and shalt believe in thine heart that God hath raised him from the dead, thou shalt be saved. For with the heart man believeth unto righteousness; and with the mouth confession is made unto salvation."

Remember Jesus' words in Matthew 12:36-37: "But I say unto you, That every idle word that men shall speak, they shall give account thereof in the day of judgment. For by thy words thou shalt be justified, and by thy words thou shalt be condemned."

You are not justified by how much fasting you do or by how many hours you spend in prayer. Jesus said you are either justified or condemned by the words that come out of your mouth. There is quite a price placed on words.

Stopping Satan With Words

Satan's No. 1 ploy is to keep your attention on the experiences of life. He will keep you trying to analyze what happened to you and why. He will try to sell you the lie so many religious people have bought—that the storms of life come on you to teach you. As long as you believe that, Satan can keep you involved in those storms and see to it that you never live the victorious life.

Satan will say to you: "You're not going to make it." If you agree with him, he will run roughshod over you. He will push you as far as he can. But I want you to realize that Satan can be stopped....with the Word of God.

When you're hit with a negative thought, speak a response. "No, Satan, the Word of God says I have authority over you. I've been made the righteousness of God through Jesus Christ and I refuse to go one step further under your influence. I will not allow you to put sickness and disease on my body any longer. You are not my god. Jesus is my Lord."

Once you make that decision and speak forth the Word of God, you must be willing to hold your ground and not change or relent in any way. Satan will challenge you, so you will have to stand firm in his face and refuse to budge 1 inch!

Put Out the Fire

"And the tongue is a fire, a world of iniquity...and [it] setteth on fire the course of nature; and it is set on fire of hell" (James 3:6). This is how the system works. Satan has been using your tongue to set on fire the course of nature against you. From the moment you were born into the world, you were trained to speak negatively about your life and circumstances around you. By using your tongue, Satan sets in motion the course of nature in your life.

Stop and listen to your everyday conversation. Train yourself to hear your own words. Much of it is so-called "casual" remarks that you make, never thinking of the effect those words are having on your life.

For instance, when cold weather first sets in, there is much talk about the flu season being just around the corner. People comment to friends about the extra doctor bills they will have to pay. This kind of remark is a product of fear—fear that sickness and disease is coming, that it is inevitable.

If asked, "Do you believe in healing?" you'd answer, "Yes of course," but your everyday conversation may negate that statement of faith. Proverbs 6:2 says you

are snared with the words of your mouth.

As you make statements of fear, doubt, unbelief, etc., the pilot light to destruction is lit; and Satan will fan the flame every way he can to make it grow. Then once he gets that fire built up around you, he will attack. To the untrained eye, it will seem that tragedy struck from out of nowhere. The first thing you do is question, "Why? Why did this happen to me?" It seems to be an unanswerable question, but there is an answer: The tongue sets on fire the course of nature, and the tongue is "set on fire of hell."

By knowing that your tongue controls the entire course of your life, you can put a stop to Satan's operation. You can control Satan by learning to control your own tongue. Though it may seem impossible, it can be done; but it requires the power of the Holy Spirit at work in your life.

Tame Your Tongue

James 3:7-8 says, "For every kind of beasts, and of birds, and of serpents, and of things in the sea, is tamed, and hath been tamed of mankind: But the tongue can no man tame; it is an unruly evil, full of deadly poison." Man can tame the wild beasts, but he cannot tame his own tongue.

This does not say that the tongue cannot be tamed. It simply says that *man* cannot tame it. The tongue cannot be tamed with the same natural power that man uses to tame animals. It takes spiritual power, and spiritual power is what every born-again believer has at his disposal. Jesus said, "My words are spirit" (John 6:63). Thank God for His written Word!

Your tongue is only an instrument. Your heart is where the key lies. Whatever is in your heart is what will come out of your mouth. If you fill your heart with God's Word, then God's Word will come out of your mouth. You can begin today setting a new standard for your life by changing the words that come out of your mouth. But first, you need to use the authority of God's Word and break the power of past words spoken.

(From: *The Power of the Tongue* by Kenneth Copeland © 1980 Kenneth Copeland)

Evening
Reflection

When Satan whispers a negative thought to you, how should you respond?

_____
_____
_____
_____
_____
_____

How can your tongue be tamed?

_____
_____
_____
_____
_____
_____

What are some negative words you regularly speak that you'll speak no more?

_____
_____
_____
_____
_____
_____

Notes:

_____
_____
_____
_____
_____
_____
_____
_____
_____
_____
_____
_____
_____
_____
_____
_____

Today's
Prayer of Faith

Father, the seed of Your Word is in my heart and being spoken out of my mouth. I see that Your will has always been for me to prosper and be in health, as my soul prospers. Thank You for what You have done for me! In Jesus' Name. Amen.

_____
_____
_____
_____
_____
_____
_____
_____
_____

REAL-LIFE TESTIMONIES
To Help Build Your Faith

Confession Produces Results

I had been suffering from sickness for about two years when I attended your KCM conference in Brighton, England. I had pain in my body all the time. For over a year I had not been able to sleep through the night because of the pain. That made it hard for me to get up in the morning to spend time with God. Even though I knew that healing belonged to me, I didn't get into faith. I was only desperate to be free from the pain, and instead of believing God, I would cry and beg Him to heal me.

When I attended your meetings in Brighton and got into the atmosphere of faith, I got courage to take my first steps of faith. I started confessing the Word when I woke up at night because of pain. I also confessed the commandment of love. I understood that I got healed 2,000 years ago at the Cross, that I am not the sick trying to get healed, but I am the healed protecting my health. When Gloria had Healing School on Saturday, I got prayed for and decided this was the day I would receive my healing. It didn't matter if I could feel it or not.

I continued confessing, and I found all the scriptures I could find in the Bible on the subject of healing. I gradually got better, eventually could sleep through the night and a little over a year after the conference, I was totally healed. Glory to God! Now I know exactly what to do if the devil attacks me with sickness again. Thank you for teaching the word of faith.

E.M.V.
Norway

Chapter Seven
Receiving Your Healing

Healed People Are People Who Receive!
by Gloria Copeland

One of the best ways to increase our capacity to receive from God is to study the accounts the Bible gives of people who were good receivers. I want to focus on four of my favorites: the woman with the issue of blood; Jairus, the synagogue ruler; the Roman centurion; and the beggar—blind Bartimaeus. Open your Bible, because I have a few passages I want you to read from today.

We find the first two accounts of good receivers in Mark 5:22-34. Their stories are so intertwined in Scripture that they are best told together. Read those verses before you continue.

First, let's look at the woman with the issue of blood. She was facing some very bad circumstances. She was not only sick, she was sick and broke. She could have easily stayed in her room and felt sorry for herself. She could have sat on her bed, crying and thinking, *If God is good, why has He let this happen to me?*

But something happened to her that made her decide not to do that. She heard and welcomed into her heart the word about Jesus. She had, no doubt, heard that He was healing people, and she believed it.

What's more, she acted on her faith. The first action she took was to open her mouth and say what she believed. Notice, she did not say what she felt or how terrible her life had been. She spoke words of faith, saying, "If I may touch but his clothes, I shall be whole" (verse 28). According to *The Amplified Bible,* she did not just say that once, either. She "kept saying" it.

Then she took the next step of faith. She left her home, in spite of the fact that it was against the Jewish law for her to be in public in her condition. She fought and pushed her way through the crowd surrounding Jesus. She reached out to touch His clothes.

Sure enough, exactly what she said happened. She was instantly healed. Other people were touching Jesus, but theirs was not the touch of faith so they were not receiving anything from Him. She was the one who was believing, speaking and acting on the word she had heard about Him, so she was the one who received! According to Jesus, it was her faith (her believing and saying) that made her whole. Jesus said, "Daughter, thy faith hath made thee whole; go in peace, and be whole of thy plague" (verse 34).

Wholehearted Faith Speaks!

Look at how Jairus, the synagogue ruler, received. We can immediately see striking similarities between his behavior and that of the woman with the issue of blood. He, too, had obviously heard the reports of Jesus' love and power and had believed them.

We also find him speaking words of faith. After telling Jesus about his sick daughter, he said, "'Come and lay Your hands on her, that she may be healed, and she will live'" (verse 23, *New King James Version*). Pay special attention to those last three words. They are not a request; they are a declaration of faith: "She will live."

Watch Jesus' response to Jairus, and you will see a clear picture of how God always responds to those who reach out to Him in faith, trusting His goodness and power. Jesus did not say, "Who do you think you are to tell Me what to do? Maybe I don't want to come to your house. Who are you to tell Me to lay My hands on someone for healing? Maybe I want to do it some other way."

No, Jesus didn't say any of those things. On the contrary, He immediately turned and went with Jairus, intending to do exactly what Jairus asked. He was easily entreated, easy to receive from.

Although the Bible does not specifically say so, I believe Jairus had to exercise great patience to receive his miracle. He had already told Jesus his daughter was at the point of death. Time was of the essence. But in spite of the critical nature of the situation, Jesus allowed an interruption. He stopped, spoke to the woman who had been healed of the issue of blood, listened to her tell the story of her illness, and

confirmed to her that her faith had made her whole.

I can just imagine how Jairus must have felt. Surely he was thinking, *Hurry up, Jesus! Can't You talk to this woman later?*

To make matters worse—much worse—by the time that incident was over, Jairus had received very bad news. Read Mark 5:35-42.

I think it is very interesting that when Jairus received news of his daughter's death, Jesus immediately said to him, "Be not afraid, only believe" (verse 36). Why was Jesus so quick and definite about that? He knew Jairus' wholehearted faith and his faith-filled words had put him in position to receive his daughter's healing. He did not want Jairus to step out of position by allowing fear to get into his heart and choke his faith. Jesus did not want Jairus to diminish his capacity to receive by speaking words of doubt and fear.

Thankfully, Jairus did exactly what Jesus said. As a result, Jesus did exactly what Jairus had said. He went to Jairus' house, took the girl by the hand, and told her to rise. She came back to life healed, just like Jairus said she would!

Jesus Changes His Plans

Some people seem to have the idea that faith offends God. Or maybe they have the idea that God doesn't want to be bothered. Religious people especially seem to get upset at the idea that anyone would be bold enough to expect God to do exactly what they asked Him to do. But the fact is, faith does not offend God; it pleases Him. Hebrews 11:6 says, "But without faith it is impossible to please him: for he that cometh to God must believe that he is, and that he is a rewarder of them that diligently seek him."

God isn't bothered by the boldness of the one who comes to Him in faith, because that boldness isn't inspired by the person's confidence in himself. It's inspired by his confidence in God—in His goodness, His love and His power.

One of the best examples of such confidence can be found in Matthew 8:5-13, in the story of the Roman centurion. Read those verses now.

Isn't that account amazing? Not only did Jesus do what this man asked Him to do, He changed His plans in accordance with the man's next request. Jesus intended to go to his house and heal the servant, but the centurion said, in essence, "No, I'd rather You not come to my house because I'm not worthy. Just speak the word and my servant will be healed."

Once again, notice the centurion put himself in position to receive, just as Jairus and the woman with the issue of blood had done. He heard and believed the word about Jesus. He spoke words of faith, saying, "My servant shall be healed" (verse 8). And he put action to his faith by coming to the Lord.

Making the Faith Connection

Our final example of good receiving is found in the healing of blind Bartimaeus. Mark 10:46-52 tells the story. Read it now.

One of my favorite things about Bartimaeus is that he refused to let the people around him discourage him. They did not have the faith in God's goodness that he had. They had such limited understanding of God's love that they thought

Jesus would not be interested in a seemingly worthless, blind beggar. But Bartimaeus had heard about Jesus. No doubt he had heard of His mercy, kindness and healing power. And he believed.

So, when the people tried to shut him up, he cried out all the louder, "Thou son of David, have mercy on me" (verse 48)! Why did he cry so loudly? Because he was convinced in his heart that if Jesus heard him, He would answer. Jesus would deliver him. This was his chance of a lifetime.

Jesus heard him and when He did, He stood still and commanded that Bartimaeus be called. Aggressive faith gets Jesus' attention.

What Bartimaeus did next was one of the most beautiful expressions of faith recorded in the New Testament. He threw off his cloak. By that act, he was making a very clear statement. He was saying, "I'm not a blind man anymore. Jesus has heard me, and I'm as good as healed!"

Notice what Jesus asked Bartimaeus next. He said, "What do you want Me to do for you?" (verse 51, *The Amplified Bible*).

Bartimaeus said boldly, "Master, let me receive my sight."

Bartimaeus was in perfect position to receive. God was looking to and fro throughout the whole earth for someone to whom He could show Himself strong...and He found Bartimaeus, full of faith, speaking and acting with great confidence in Jesus' goodness and power. The connection was made and Jesus said, "Go your way; your faith has healed you" (verse 52, *The Amplified Bible*).

I want you to be impressed by Jesus'

goodness and how willing He was to express that goodness. Whatever those who came to Him for help said, He said. Jesus acted on *their* words! He, just like His Father, was easy to receive from.

The woman with the issue of blood said, "If I only touch His garments, I shall be restored to health" (Mark 5:28, *The Amplified Bible*). The moment she touched them, she received her healing.

Whatever the centurion asked Jesus, He was willing to do, so that the centurion's desire could be answered and the servant healed.

Jesus asked Bartimaeus, "What can I do for you?" Bartimaeus told Him what he wanted and Jesus said, "Your faith has made you whole." What Bartimaeus said, Jesus did. He immediately received his sight and followed Jesus.

Hebrews 13:8 says, "Jesus Christ the same yesterday, and today, and for ever." Jesus and the Father are still going about doing good and healing all who will receive. "The Lord is good to all: and his tender mercies are over all his works" (Psalm 145:9).

Jesus is saying the same thing to you today that He said to Bartimaeus. He is asking all who would look to Him in faith, "What do you want Me to do for you?"

(From: Blessed Beyond Measure by Gloria Copeland © 2004 Gloria Copeland)

Morning Reflection

What made each of these believers good receivers?

_____

_____

_____

_____

_____

_____

_____

Which receiver can you best identify with and why?

_____

_____

_____

_____

_____

_____

_____

What do these examples show us about the ease of receiving from Jesus?

_____

_____

_____

_____

_____

_____

_____

_____

_____

_____

_____

_____

Today's Connection Points

(•) *Healing Praise* CD: "'Tis So Sweet to Trust in Jesus" (Track 4)

Receive your healing today as you focus on trusting in Jesus—in everything you say and do.

(•) *Healing Scriptures* CD: Track 10

Listen to miraculous healings from the Bible as you get the Word into your heart so it comes out of your mouth!

Acts 19:11-12, 28:8-9, 10:38; Galatians 3:13-14; 2 Timothy 3:10-11; Hebrews 4:14-15;
James 5:13-16

(•) DVD: "The Prayer of Faith" (Chapter 7)

Learn how the prayer of faith includes salvation *and* healing, in this powerful message from Gloria.

Make a faith connection.
Put yourself in position to receive today!

Notes:

_____
_____
_____
_____
_____
_____
_____
_____
_____
_____
_____
_____
_____
_____
_____
_____
_____

Making a Declaration of Faith
by Kenneth Copeland

In the fall of 2004, when a disk blew out in my back, I had to take the final stand against this attack I'd been dealing with for several years. The Lord showed me how I had gotten in such bad shape and He gave me knowledge, understanding and wisdom in how my body would be restored.

I have had faith. Faith to preach, to lay hands on the sick, to believe for financial breakthrough. Faith for my family, for the ministry and for my Partners and Friends. But the Lord let me know in no uncertain terms that, as far as my personal health was concerned, I was living on leftover faith.

And because of His great love, not just for me but for you, too, He took me right back to the basics of receiving to bring my restoration.

He took me back to the foundational principles that I had been teaching for more than 38 years. The last stand for my healing began with a basic declaration of faith. My family gathered together to declare God's Word for my healing, my ministry staff joined us, my personal physicians came into agreement with us, and my Partners prayed in faith with us.

Shortly, my health was completely restored. Praise God! And that same stand we took together for my healing is the action we must take for any situation in our lives that makes us in any way less effective for the ministry and work to which God has called us. Restoration always comes by the Word of God, whether the situation involves healing, deliverance, finances, emotions, broken relationships at home, in our churches or businesses.

When it comes to receiving from God, the declaration of faith is sure! The Lord has proved it to Gloria and me over and over again, day in and day out, since the day we made our first declaration that Jesus is Lord of our lives (Romans 10:9).

Below, I've outlined the steps to the declaration of faith we've used to get through the hardest of times. As we take these simple steps, we give the Lord all the room He needs to bring restoration to every challenging circumstance of life—whether the problem is our own doing or a work of the enemy.

From the day each of us begins living with Jesus as Lord, the key to restoration and wholeness in every area of life is the same: "For with the heart man believeth unto righteousness; and with the mouth confession is made unto salvation" (Romans 10:10).

As you stand to receive your healing, know that Gloria and I are in agreement with you for your complete restoration!

Five Steps to Receiving From God

Based on God's Word in Hebrews 4:12-16, here are the five steps we've used to receive our complete restoration.

1. **Present the Promises (Present Your Case).**
   "For the word of God is quick, and powerful, and sharper than any twoedged sword, piercing even to the dividing asunder of soul and spirit, and of the joints and marrow, and is a discerner of the thoughts and intents of the heart" (verse 12).

   - Go to the Word of God and find the scriptures that fit your situation. (Romans 10:17)

   - Ask the Holy Spirit to show you the promises He desires you to apply. (Romans 8:1-16)

2. **Pray and Worship God.**
   "Neither is there any creature that is not manifest in his sight: but all things are naked and opened unto the eyes of him with whom we have to do" (verse 13).

   - Humble yourself before the Lord. (James 4:10)
   - Lay the promises before Him. (1 John 5:15)
   - Hear His wisdom and the instruction of the Holy Spirit. (John 16:13)

3. **Make Your Petition.**
   "Seeing then that we have a great high priest, that is passed into the heavens, Jesus the Son of God..." (verse 14).

   - Write your petition out as your Word-based declaration of faith. (Philippians 4:6)
   - Present it to the High Priest of your confession, Jesus.

4. **Prepare to Receive.**
   "Let us hold fast our profession [confession]" (verse 14).

   - Let faith and patience work together in your life. (James 1:3-4)

5. **Praise God for the Manifestation of Victory!** "Let us therefore come boldly unto the throne of grace...and find grace to help in time of need" (verse 16).

   - Let every request be accompanied by your thanksgiving to the Lord for His faithfulness to fulfill His promises. (Philippians 4:6; 2 Corinthians 1:20)

Take time out right now to make a declaration of faith for your healing. Then get ready...because your victory is nigh!

(From: *Declaration of Faith* brochure, Kenneth Copeland Ministries, product # 70-0729)

Evening Reflection

How does a declaration of faith set your faith in motion to receive?

_____

_____

_____

_____

_____

_____

_____

What promises from the Word directly minister to your situation?

_____

_____

_____

_____

_____

_____

Write your personal petition below:

_____

_____

_____

_____

_____

_____

_____

_____

_____

_____

Notes:

_____
_____
_____
_____
_____
_____
_____
_____
_____
_____
_____
_____

Today's
Prayer of Faith

*Father, as I begin to seek You regarding my health, I ask
that You help me by Your Holy Spirit to receive Your Word.
If I have any areas of unbelief, I am asking You to show
me and help me with those as well. Thank You that You
love me and that You are with me always! In Jesus' Name.
Amen.*

_____
_____
_____
_____
_____
_____
_____
_____
_____

REAL-LIFE TESTIMONIES
To Help Build Your Faith

What Would a Healed Woman Be Doing?

I'd had problems with my back for over 23 years. In 1993 an MRI confirmed I had three herniated disks. My back had become so sensitive to movement, a sneeze could put me in bed.

One day after a sneeze, my husband made me a bed in the living room so I could be with him and the kids. I had your broadcast on. Gloria was teaching on healing and telling people to do what they couldn't do before, by faith.

I asked God, "How can I tell my body to be healed when I know what the report said?" I heard the Lord say, *The same Spirit that raised Jesus from the dead has quickened your mortal body—that Spirit is your authority to tell your body to be healed!* So I told my body it had to respond to the authority within me and be healed!

When I asked God what a healed woman would be doing right now, He said, *She'd be doing her dishes.* So I got up from my bed, all bent over, barely able to take steps, and walked to my kitchen sink. I began doing my dishes and before I was through, I was standing upright and still am to this day!

Thank you. It would take many tablets to tell how KCM has helped our family in our walk with God, but suffice it to say, God is GOOD!

L.E.
Texas

Chapter Eight
Standing for Results

Having Done All...Stand
by Gloria Copeland

As you put God's prescription for health to work in your life—from putting the Word in your heart, to speaking it out, to receiving—don't be discouraged if you don't see immediate results. Although many times healing comes instantly, there are also times when it takes place more gradually.

So don't let lingering symptoms cause you to doubt. After all, when you go to the doctor, you don't always feel better right away. The medication you're given often takes some time before it begins to work. But you don't allow the delay to discourage you. You follow the doctor's orders and expect to feel better soon. Release that same kind of confidence in God's medicine. Realize that the moment you begin to take it, the healing process begins. Keep your expectancy high and make up your mind to continue standing on the Word until you can see and feel the total physical effects of God's healing power. Really, you are "treating" your spirit, which is the source of supernatural life and health for your physical body.

When the devil whispers words of doubt and unbelief to you, suggesting that the Word is not working, deal with those thoughts immediately. Cast them down (see 2 Corinthians 10:5).

Stop right where you are and say out loud, "No. I cast you down, you evil imagination. Devil, I rebuke you. I bind you from my mind. I will not believe your lies. God has sent His Word to heal me, and His Word never fails. That Word went to work in my body the instant I believed it, so as far as I am concerned, my days of sickness are over. I declare that Jesus bore my sickness, weakness and pain and I am forever free."

Then, having done all to stand, stand until your healing is fully manifest (see Ephesians 6:12-14). Steadfastly hold your ground. Don't waver. James 1:6-8 says, "He that wavereth is like a wave of the sea driven with the wind and tossed.... Let not that man think that he shall receive any thing of the Lord. A double minded man is unstable in all his ways."

If your condition is serious, you may also have to resist the temptation to worry. The devil will try to use anxiety over your situation to choke the Word in your heart and make it unfruitful (Mark 4:19), but don't let him succeed. Just trust God, "casting all your care upon him; for he careth for you" (1 Peter 5:7) and constantly keep in mind these wonderful words from Hebrews:

He Who promised is reliable (sure) and faithful to His word.... Do not, therefore, fling away your fearless confidence, for it carries a great and glorious compensation of reward. For you have need of steadfast patience and endurance, so that you may perform and fully accomplish the will of God, and thus receive and carry away [and enjoy to the full] what is promised (Hebrews 10:23, 35-36, *The Amplified Bible*).

Above all, keep your attention trained on the Word—not on lingering symptoms. Be like Abraham who "considered not his own body" (Romans 4:19). Instead of focusing on your circumstances, focus on what God has said to you. Develop an inner image of yourself with your healing fully manifest. See yourself well. See yourself whole. See yourself healed in every way.

Since what you keep before your eyes and in your ears determines what you will believe in your heart and what you will act on, make the Word your No. 1 priority. Attend to it—and it will attend to you!

(From: *God's Prescription for Divine Health* by Gloria Copeland © 1995 Eagle Mountain International Church Inc. aka Kenneth Copeland Ministries)

How do you "cast down" thoughts of doubt?

_____
_____
_____
_____
_____
_____

What does it mean to "stand"?

_____
_____
_____
_____
_____

What does God say we should do with our cares?

_____

_____

_____

_____

_____

_____

_____

_____

_____

_____

Today's
Connection Points

- *Healing Praise* CD: "I Sing Praises to Your Name," "I Stand in Awe" (Tracks 5-6)

  As you stand strong for your healing, stand in awe of the One who has made you whole!

- *Healing Scriptures* CD: Track 12

  Stand for your results as you stir up your faith with today's healing scriptures.

  Colossians 2:13-15

- DVD: "Speak the Word" (Chapter 8)

  Learn how God *did* what three people *said*...in faith.

 Stand strong, knowing that your healing was accomplished at Calvary.

Resist all doubt and worry—cast your cares on Him!

Notes:

_____

_____

_____

_____

_____

_____

_____

_____

_____

_____

_____

_____

_____

_____

_____

_____

Receiving Communion as You Stand

by Kenneth Copeland

As you stand for your healing, receiving Communion is a key element to staying strong and partaking of all Jesus has provided for us.

When a believer partakes of the Lord's Supper, he should do so with full understanding of its significance. Communion, to many people, has become only a religious observance. But it has a much deeper meaning than that.

The Communion table is an emblem of Jesus' sacrifice for us. "Jesus took bread, and blessed it, and brake it…and said, Take, eat; this is my body. And he took the cup, and gave thanks, and gave it to them, saying, Drink ye all of it; for this is my blood of the new testament, which is shed for many for the remission of sins" (Matthew 26:26-28).

Primarily, the Church has centered its attention on the wine as an emblem of Jesus' blood that was shed for sin. We take the emblem of blood and say, "Thank God, we are delivered from sin," and that's true! Praise God for it! But the blood is only half of Communion. The bread is an emblem of Jesus' body that was broken for us. The emblem of His body is just as important as the emblem of His blood.

According to Isaiah 53:4-5, Jesus' sacrifice covered *every area* of man's existence. He bore spiritual torment for our sins, mental distress for our worry, care and fear as well as physical pain for our sickness and disease. The stripes He bore were for our healing. "With His stripes we are healed" (Isaiah 53:5).

God gave *everything He had* to redeem mankind from the curse. For us to receive only part of His sacrifice is an insult to Him.

When we receive Communion, we are receiving His body and His blood. Every time we partake, we should examine ourselves closely according to 1 Corinthians 11:28-29. "But let a man examine himself, and so let him eat of that bread, and drink of that cup. For he that eateth and drinketh unworthily, eateth and drinketh damnation to himself, not discerning the Lord's body." There is much more involved in receiving Communion than most Christians realize.

God instituted the Lord's Supper for a reason. When you receive it, you should be ready to partake of everything Jesus' sacrifice provided—salvation, peace of mind, healing, total prosperity. In the past, we missed the full meaning of Communion by not completely judging ourselves when we partook of it.

We have been ready to receive His

blood and quick to judge ourselves and repent where sin is concerned. But what about His body? It was broken for us. It was bruised for us. The stripes laid on Jesus' back were for our healing. So at Communion, we should judge ourselves where sickness is concerned as well. Jesus purchased our *healing* at Calvary just as He purchased our salvation.

With this in mind, when we partake of Communion we should say, "Lord, it's not right that I should suffer from sickness and disease. I judge it now as being from Satan, and I reject it. I refuse to receive it any longer. I partake of the sacrifice of Your body, and I receive the healing You provided, in Jesus' Name."

When you partake of Communion, make a point of judging yourself to the fullest extent. Don't just receive it halfway. *Accept everything Jesus' sacrifice provided.* If you don't examine yourself—if you receive Communion just as a religious exercise—you will be eating and drinking unworthily, not discerning the Lord's body. Paul wrote, "For this cause many are weak and sickly among you, and many sleep" (1 Corinthians 11:30).

When the first Passover was instituted, God instructed Moses to kill a lamb, spread its blood over the door, and then roast the lamb and eat all of it. Any that remained was to be burned away. That sacrificial lamb was completely consumed! Jesus, as the Lamb of God, was the supreme sacrifice under the Abrahamic Covenant. When you partake of His sacrifice, do not take only part of it. Receive *all* Jesus did for you! Consume it completely!

When you receive the Lord's Supper, partake of it like the children of Israel did, "with your loins girded, your shoes on your feet, and your staff in your hand; and ye shall eat it in haste: it is the Lord's passover" (Exodus 12:11). They were ready to go. They ate in faith, ready to receive their deliverance before they ate!

No matter what you may be faced with—sin, sickness, a weight problem, worry, strife, old habits—you can be delivered through properly receiving the Lord's Supper. The body and blood of Jesus covers *every area* of your existence. By discerning His body and judging yourself before Him, you can receive your deliverance. Place yourself before God and receive Communion—like the children of Israel—ready to receive your deliverance!

You don't have to wait until you go to church to receive Communion. Receive it at home. Get up an hour earlier in the morning every now and then. Take the time to put yourself before God over the Communion table. It will be time well spent. I guarantee it!

(From: *How to Receive Communion* by Kenneth Copeland © 1982 International Church of the Word of Faith Inc. now known as Eagle Mountain International Church Inc. aka Kenneth Copeland Ministries)

What is the full significance of the cup during Communion?

_____
_____
_____
_____
_____

What is the full significance of the bread during Communion?

_____
_____
_____
_____
_____

How does taking Communion help you while you are standing for your healing?

_____
_____
_____
_____

Notes:

_____
_____
_____
_____
_____
_____
_____
_____
_____
_____
_____

Today's
Prayer of Faith

*Father, I know You have already made salvation and
healing available to me by Your Word. I choose now to
receive from You all that You have for me. I choose to
believe You, rather than my circumstances. Thank You for
helping me to stand strong. In Jesus' Name. Amen.*

_____
_____
_____
_____
_____
_____
_____
_____
_____
_____
_____
_____
_____
_____
_____
_____
_____
_____

Healing Scriptures Restore Heart

Thank you so much for the healing material you recently sent me. It was an answer to prayer. I emailed you a few weeks ago about my 19-year-old son. He had been having chest pains and shortness of breath. After having several tests, it appeared to his doctor that the left side of his heart was not beating correctly and too slowly. He was referred to a cardiologist.

You started praying, and my church was praying, as well as other friends. I was looking for all the healing scriptures I could find when your *How to Receive Healing* packet came. I started quoting the scriptures about healing and fear, and my son was believing and saying the scriptures.

When we went to the doctor, the physician's assistant said his heart was beating and pumping as normally as a well-trained athlete. We are so thankful to God for this miracle, because we believe if we had not stood in faith and had all that prayer backing us up, and most important, if we had given in to the spirit of fear that was pressing in on us, the outcome could have been different. So, from the bottom of our hearts, thank you!

S.F.
Texas

Chapter Nine
Things That Block Healing

A Living Sacrifice
by Gloria Copeland

God never holds out on us. His will is that all men be healed—and that includes you! Jesus purchased your healing at the same time He purchased your redemption from sin (Isaiah 53:4-5). So health is just as available to you as salvation.

When we fail to receive something He's promised, we can always be assured that the problem lies with us and not with Him. There are, however, several things that might be preventing us from receiving it.

1. Disobedience

Jesus teaches us that our commandment is to walk in love (Matthew 22:37-39). We are to love God with all our hearts and to love each other. If we don't do that, we're in disobedience—and that opens the door to the enemy and hinders the life flow. Disobedience comes in the form of wrong words, traditions of men, anger, bitterness, grief, fear, envy and jealousy. These things can adversely affect our health and our ability to receive from God. They are not the result of love.

Also, remember that Galatians 5:6 says faith works by love. So if you want your faith to prevail over sickness and disease, you have to operate in love. Read 1 Corinthians 13:4-8 and find out how God's kind of love behaves. After all, love is not a feeling. It's an action. So start acting in love and your healing won't be far behind.

2. Unbelief

In Mark 11:24, Jesus tells us what is required for us to receive from God. He said, "What things soever ye desire, when ye pray, believe that ye receive them, and ye shall have them."

Most people are only willing to believe they've received healing after they can *see* or *feel* the results. But according to that scripture, you must believe you receive it *when you pray*. When you believe by faith that you have what you ask for, then the healing will come.

3. Sin

First John 3:22 says we receive whatever we ask of God because we do those things that are pleasing in His sight. Living a life free from habitual sin and rebellion causes us to have confidence in our hearts toward God. And confidence toward God is an essential part of the operation of faith.

4. Unforgiveness

This is perhaps the greatest hindrance to healing. That's why immediately after giving instructions about faith, Jesus said, "And when ye stand praying, forgive, if ye have aught against any: that your Father also which is in heaven may forgive you your trespasses. But if ye do not forgive, neither will your Father which is in heaven forgive your trespasses" (Mark 11:25-26).

Notice the words *when ye stand praying*. Don't wait. As soon as someone offends you, forgive immediately and your prayers will never be hindered.

Deny Yourself

Now, how do we get to the place where we are manifesting the fruit of the spirit and not the works of the flesh? Jesus said, "If any man will come after me, let him deny himself, and take up his cross, and follow me" (Matthew 16:24). Jesus came to the earth and lived in a natural body just like yours and mine. He was tempted by the weakness of His flesh, *but He never sinned* (Hebrews 2:16-18). By His Spirit indwelling us, He is able to come to our aid when we are tempted. *Our cross* is to deny ourselves the luxury of walking after the flesh. We must disregard our own interests to walk in the spirit.

Romans 12:1-2 talks about crucifying the flesh. It says:

I beseech you therefore, brethren, by the mercies of God, that ye present your bodies a living sacrifice, holy, acceptable unto God, which is your reasonable service. And be not conformed to this world: but be ye transformed by the renewing of your mind, that ye may prove what is that good, and acceptable, and perfect, will of God.

You do not have to fight the war between your flesh and spirit. Instead, offer yourself as a living sacrifice to God. Lay down your own desires to fulfill His. Your inner man will rise to the occasion with the help of the Holy Spirit. You will no longer desire the things you used to because you are retraining yourself to the things of the spirit.

God is calling us to give ourselves. He is calling us to live to please Him. Jesus said, "If any man serve me, him will my Father honour" (John 12:26). We cannot serve the flesh and serve Jesus at the same time.

We must make a *decision*. Are we going to please ourselves or please the Father? Are we going to go after carnal desires, or are we going to fulfill the will of God? We are to crucify our flesh and bring it into obedience to God.

To crucify the flesh is your *reasonable* service. You were bought with a precious price. Jesus bought you with the crucifixion of His own flesh. He is asking you to take up that same cross daily. Follow Him. Glorify God in your body. Doing so is acceptable and well-pleasing to Him.

He said you would be transformed. Romans 8:29 says, "For whom he did foreknow, he also did predestinate to be conformed to the image of his Son, that he might be the firstborn among many brethren." Giving the Holy Spirit opportunity to bear you up in your weakness causes you to be transformed into the image of Jesus! If you are walking in the spirit when temptation comes, you won't give in to it.

If we make our bodies a living sacrifice, we will be transformed. That means we will change on the *outside!* When we walk in the spirit of life in Christ Jesus, the law of sin and death has to fall at our feet. Satan has no avenue into our lives.

Live to Please God

When you live to please God, you will not be squeezed into the world's mold. You'll be transformed into the image of Jesus!

Today is the day to offer your body as a living sacrifice to God. Before you do another thing, lift your hands to God and yield yourself as a living sacrifice, holy and acceptable to Him. You'll never be the same!

If you are consistent in these four areas, you can be confident that your healing will come. So just keep standing in faith (Ephesians 6:12-13) and you will receive!

(From: the *Believer's Voice of Victory* magazine, January 1986, April 2004, July 2006 and various 2003 meetings)

What are some things that can block healing?

_____

_____

_____

_____

_____

_____

_____

_____

What does Romans 12 mean when it calls offering our bodies as a living sacrifice our "reasonable service"?

_____

_____

_____

_____

_____

_____

_____

What are some areas that might be blocking your healing? What will you do about them?

_____
_____
_____
_____
_____
_____
_____
_____
_____
_____
_____
_____

Today's
Connection Points

- ### *Healing Praise* CD: "Give Thanks" (Track 1)

  As you commit to walking in love, focus on giving thanks to Love, Himself, the One who has redeemed you!

- ### *Healing Scriptures* CD: Track 11

  Hear these life-changing scriptures about how Jesus bore your sicknesses for you!

  1 Peter 2:24; 1 John 3:7-8; 3 John 2; Luke 6:6-10, 8:41-52, 54-56

- ### DVD: "Have Mercy" (Chapter 9)

  Enjoy a great testimony followed by Gloria's continued teaching on biblical examples of those who received.

 Examine your life to see if there is anything blocking your healing.

Choose to walk in love and live to please God, today!

Notes:

_____
_____
_____
_____
_____
_____
_____
_____
_____
_____
_____
_____
_____
_____
_____
_____
_____

Living Love-Conscious

by Kenneth Copeland

There's no better way to conquer the things that block healing than living a life of love. The entire New Covenant—all that it involves—is wrapped up in love.

Till we all come in the unity of the faith, and of the knowledge of the Son of God, unto a perfect man, unto the measure of the stature of the fulness of Christ: That we henceforth be no more children, tossed to and fro, and carried about with every wind of doctrine, by the sleight of men, and cunning craftiness, whereby they lie in wait to deceive; but speaking the truth in love, may grow up into him in all things, which is the head, even Christ: From whom the whole body fitly joined together and compacted by that which every joint supplieth, according to the effectual working in the measure of every part, maketh increase of the body unto the edifying of itself in love (Ephesians 4:13-16).

According to God's Word, we can walk in perfected love while we are here in this earth. God is love so love itself is already perfect; but we have to allow God to express His perfection in our lives. We do that by keeping His Word.

The world's systems and ideas are accepted as the norm, but they are *not* the norm. God's Word is the norm and the standard by which we are to live. Man was created to function on God's level. Adam walked on that level in the Garden of Eden, but when he disobeyed God, he fell from his position of fellowship and oneness with God. It took Jesus coming to earth as a man to reclaim the authority Adam had given over to Satan. Today, every born-again believer can live on that supernatural level through the power of God's love, by the Holy Spirit.

I've heard the love walk described this way: "To walk in love, to live in this God kind of love, is like a man walking in a dense, early morning fog. He walks in it until his clothes are saturated with moisture, until the brim of his hat drips with water." You can walk in the love of God to the point that your whole being is saturated with love. Every word you speak drips with love and everyone you come in contact with is affected by that love. Hallelujah!

Become Love-Conscious

In studying the love of God, you must remember this: Walking in love is not just "being nice." Jesus was Love manifested in the flesh, but there were times when He didn't appear to be "nice." One time He called the people serpents and vipers (Matthew 23:33). Another time He called a Syrophenician woman a dog (Mark 7:27). It didn't sound very sweet, but His words were effective. They got her attention and penetrated her unbelief. When He got through to her, she quit begging, looked Him straight in the face, and said, "... yet the dogs under the table eat of the children's crumbs" (Mark 7:28). She let Him know that she wasn't leaving without the deliverance of her daughter. Jesus then said, "For this saying go thy way; the devil is gone out of thy daughter" (verse 29).

Love is a way of life—a life of being love-conscious instead of self-conscious. If you are not being love-conscious, you will always take the selfish route. Being love-conscious does not come automatically; it requires training. The Word says we are to practice love. "If we love one another, God dwelleth in us, and his love is perfected in us" (1 John 4:12). As we love one another, God's love is perfected in us.

The Commitment

Few have decided to live in that realm of the miraculous—receiving all God has for them, renewing their minds with the Word and separating themselves from the carnal ways of the world:

I beseech you therefore, brethren, by the mercies of God, that ye present your bodies a living sacrifice, holy, acceptable unto God, which is your reasonable service. And be not conformed to this world: but be ye transformed by the renewing of your mind, that ye may prove what is that good, and acceptable, and perfect, will of God (Romans 12:1-2).

This is the committed believer—one who has made the decision to be a holy vessel of honor, sanctified, and meet for the Master's use, prepared unto every good work (2 Timothy 2:21). A born-again child of God is bone of His bone and flesh of His flesh, joined one spirit with the Lord (Ephesians 5:30; 1 Corinthians 6:17).

Standing in Full Measure

This is the ultimate realm of God's power and love—the place where all phases of ministry come together and operate at their fullest capacity.

God has been dealing with me about walking in the fullness of the gifts of the Spirit. In my estimation, the best I have seen of spiritual gifts in operation has fallen short of what God wants to do.

I have been very blessed to see great and miraculous happenings, both in church congregations and out in the streets. I have seen the power of God in operation, but have never yet walked away satisfied that God did *everything* He wanted to do. The time is coming and now is at hand for the fullness of the gifts of the Spirit to operate, for God to do what He has been wanting to do all these years. Jesus said, "He that believeth on me, the works that I do shall he do also; and greater works than these shall he do; because I go unto my Father" (John

14:12). The things I am going to share with you now are the things that will put us in position to walk in that fullness of greater works.

We haven't reached that place yet, but we're headed that way now. We have finally come to the place where many of us are joining together and worshiping God in unity, "Till we all come in the unity of the faith, and of the knowledge of the Son of God, unto a perfect man, unto the measure of the stature of the fulness of Christ" (Ephesians 4:13). That is one of the most important steps that has to happen.

The New Breed

Our job is to walk in love toward one another and walk in this magnificent realm of the miraculous. "Speaking the truth in love, (we) may grow up into him in all things, which is the head, even Christ: from whom the whole body fitly joined together and compacted by that which every joint supplieth, according to the effectual working in the measure of every part, maketh increase of the body unto the edifying of itself in love" (Ephesians 4:15-16).

In the Greek text, the word *edify* means "to charge," as you would "charge" a battery. As we edify one another in love, we pump one another full of power! By speaking the truth in love to each other, we grow up into Him in all things and walk the earth in full stature as believers, continually building each other up with the Word.

Jesus is not coming back for a weak, sickly church that has been defeated and beaten down by Satan. No, praise God, we are going out of here in a blaze of glory!

You can walk in the realm of the miraculous, using the authority of God; but you will never do it until you put God's Word first place in your life and walk in love. That is the realm of the miraculous!

In Deuteronomy 28, the Word says, "And it shall come to pass, if thou shalt hearken diligently unto the voice of the Lord thy God, to observe and to do all his commandments (now, the love commandment is the only one to observe and do: John 15:12; Romans 13:10) which I command thee this day...all these blessings shall come on thee, and overtake thee..." (verses 1-14). Then you will be walking by faith on the highest level there is. God's miraculous power will operate in you, and you will see great and mighty things take place.

You will be counted among "the new breed" that shall go forth to the world. You shall no longer walk as other Gentiles walk in the vanity of their minds; but you shall walk in love *even as* Jesus walked—men and women knowing their full rights and privileges in Christ Jesus. You shall rise up, entirely healed and whole, proclaiming the mighty Name of Jesus, and preparing the way of the Lord's coming!

(From: *Walking in the Realm of the Miraculous: Love—The Ultimate Plan of God's Power* © 1980 Kenneth Copeland)

Evening Reflection

What does it mean to be "love-conscious"?

_____

_____

_____

_____

_____

_____

_____

_____

_____

How do love and the gifts of the Spirit work together?

_____

_____

_____

_____

_____

_____

_____

_____

_____

How do you edify others in love?

_____

_____

_____

_____

_____

_____

_____

_____

_____

Notes:

_____
_____
_____
_____
_____
_____
_____
_____
_____
_____
_____
_____
_____

Today's
Prayer of Faith

Thank You, Father, for helping me to escape the corruption in this present world by Your divine nature that is in me. I choose to operate in the life that You have given me, and to let love rule in my heart. Thank You that I am healed! In Jesus' Name. Amen.

_____
_____
_____
_____
_____
_____
_____

Healed by Jesus

By the stripes of Jesus, I was healed! I wrote to your ministry not long ago and asked you to pray for my healing. I was diagnosed with tuberculosis of the left lung. You sent me a letter, along with a prayer and scripture that I could speak out. I did it several times a day. Then in prayer, I got the instruction about what would help me get the victory in this situation. I continued taking treatment with the Word of God. After the second week, X-rays showed that I was completely well!

I.R.
Ukraine

Chapter Ten
Living a Long, Healthy Life

Live Long, Live Strong!

by Gloria Copeland

"With long life will I satisfy him, and show him my salvation" (Psalm 91:16).

The Bible has a lot to say about God's will concerning our lives here on the earth—how we are to live and for how long. God has a good, long life planned for us. But without that revelation, when we reach 60 or 70, we may start winding down and getting ready to go.

God never meant for us to die young. It's His will for us to live out the full number of our days. Traditionally, Psalm 90:10 has been quoted in regard to man's life ex-pectancy. It says: "The days of our years are threescore years and ten (70 years)—or even, if by reason of strength, fourscore years (80 years)..." *(The Amplified Bible)*. But what most people don't realize is that reading this verse alone is taking it out of context. A footnote to Psalm 90 in *The Amplified Bible* explains:

This psalm is credited to Moses, who is interceding with God to remove the curse which made it necessary for every Israelite over twenty years of age (when they rebelled against God at Kadesh-barnea) to die before reaching

the promised land (Num. 14:26-35). Moses says most of them are dying at seventy years of age. *This number has often been mistaken as a set span of life for all mankind. It was not intended to refer to anyone except those Israelites under the curse during that particular forty years. Seventy years never has been the average span of life for humanity.* When Jacob, the father of the twelve tribes, had reached 130 years (Gen. 47:9), he complained that he had not attained to the years of his immediate ancestors. In fact, Moses himself lived to be 120 years old, Aaron 123, Miriam several years older, and Joshua 110 years of age. Note as well that in the Millennium a person dying at 100 will still be thought a child (Isa. 65:20).

Here we learn that the Israelites who died at 70 were living under the curse caused by disobedience. According to Galatians 3:13, Jesus has redeemed us from the curse, being made a curse for us. If we have made Jesus our Lord, freedom from all the conditions the curse causes belongs to us—that includes sickness, destruction and early death.

So don't have the mindset that you should only live to be 70. What God actually said about man's life span is found in Genesis 6:3: "And the Lord said, My spirit shall not always strive with man, for that he also is flesh: *yet his days shall be an hundred and twenty years.*"

Think about it. That means at 60 you are just middle-aged. That's not the time to start slowing down. Instead stand on this scripture and others like Psalm 103:2-5: "Bless the Lord...who healeth all thy diseases; who redeemeth thy life from destruction...who satisfieth thy mouth with good things; so that thy youth is renewed like the eagle's." Be determined to enjoy to the fullest the many productive years the Lord has promised you.

Live Long...by the Book

Like every other blessing, there are conditions to living a long life. Psalm 91 is a picture of the person who receives this blessing.

He that dwelleth in the secret place of the most High shall abide under the shadow of the Almighty. I will say of the Lord, He is my refuge and my fortress: my God; in him will I trust. Surely he shall deliver thee from the snare of the fowler, and from the noisome pestilence. He shall cover thee with his feathers, and under his wings shalt thou trust: his truth shall be thy shield and buckler. Thou shalt not be afraid for the terror by night; nor for the arrow that flieth by day; nor for the pestilence that walketh in darkness; nor for the destruction that wasteth at noonday. A thousand shall fall at thy side, and ten thousand at thy right hand; but it shall not come nigh thee. Only with thine eyes shalt thou behold and see the reward of the wicked. Because thou hast made the Lord, which is my refuge, even the most High, thy habitation; there shall no evil befall thee, neither shall any plague come nigh thy dwelling. For he shall give his angels charge over thee, to keep thee in all thy ways. They shall bear thee up in their hands, lest thou dash thy foot against a stone. Thou shalt tread upon the lion and adder: the young lion and the dragon shalt thou trample under feet. Because he hath set his love upon me, therefore will I deliver him: I will set him on high, because he hath known my name. He shall call upon me, and I will answer him: I will be with him in trouble; I will deliver him, and honour him. *With long life will I satisfy him, and show him my salvation.*

The person this is talking about loves God and stays connected to Him. He doesn't fear, but trusts the Lord to be his refuge, and says so. The truth of God's Word is his shield and buckler. He dwells or abides under the shadow of the Almighty in obedience, and God shows him His salvation. The word *salvation* means "material and temporal deliverance from danger and apprehension, preservation, pardon, restoration, healing, wholeness and soundness."

God will satisfy you with good things, including healing, protection and long life when you are living and abiding in Him.

Keep Doing God's Will

For years I heard Kenneth Hagin say you ought to live 70 or 80 years, and if you're not satisfied, live awhile longer. He proved that to be true. He passed 80 and just kept going until he finished his work.

A commentary on Psalm 90 in the *Tehillim** says until Moses reached 80, like other men he was growing weaker. But look what happened to him then. "When he reached the age of 80, Moses received an extraordinary infusion of youthful energy and vitality, because at that time he was chosen to lead the Jewish people out of Egypt, to receive the Torah, and to lead the Jews to the Promised Land. This divine mission so invigorated him that his health and strength remained undiminished until the moment of his death."

Deuteronomy 34:7 says, "And Moses was an hundred and twenty years old when he died: his eye was not dim, nor his natural force abated."

Just as He did with Moses, God can give you a new assignment at any time. So if you have noticed that you've been slowing down because you're getting a little older, double up on the Word. Let the Word be made spirit and life to you (John 6:63). And get involved with

what God is doing. That's the best way to live a long, productive life.

Acts 1:1-2 in the *New Living Translation* says, "Jesus began to do and teach until the day he ascended...." That's my plan too—to do and teach until I ascend! I encourage you to do the same. Live long and live strong—stay well and stay here as long as God has something worthwhile for you to do.

You Don't Have to Be Sick

One woman wrote to us and asked, "If I keep getting healed, how am I ever going to die?" The best way for your body to die is for your spirit to just leave. You don't have to be evicted—forced out by sickness, disease or accident. God can call you out and say, *Come home. Come on up here.* You can simply pass over from this side to the other side, from earth to heaven. I get excited just thinking about it. Glory to God!

You don't ever have to be sick. God's best is for you to live in divine health every day, but He is also eager to heal. John G. Lake said, "Divine healing is the removal by the power of God of the disease that has come upon the body. But divine health is to live day by day, hour by hour in touch with God so that the life of God flows into the body just as the life of God flows into the mind or flows into the spirit."

You live in divine health by staying in continual contact with the Word of God and the Spirit of God. In fact, the way to be free in every area of life is to attach yourself to God.

It's your responsibility to stay well and whole. You do that with the Word of God and by resisting the devil. Go to the Bible and find out the truth. Realize that healing belongs to you and stand in faith for it. Rebuke symptoms when they try to come. Say, "No, you're not coming here, in the Name of Jesus. I'm healed by the stripes of Jesus."

When the devil tries to crowd your mind with dark thoughts about your life being cut short, rebuke them. Replace those thoughts with the promises of God. Speak the Word out loud in faith. Remember Psalm 91 says the person who makes the Lord his refuge, the one who receives protection and deliverance, has to *say so*.

Obey Natural Laws, Too

God didn't make your physical body to fail. He made your physical body to sustain itself when given the right food and the right conditions. He created your body to stay well and live to be an old age.

And if that's your goal, you'll need to determine that. Regardless of what ailments your relatives have had, they don't need to affect you. Don't look at your family history. You are born of God. Now you're part of His family. You can take the Word of God and stop any unwanted, hereditary tendencies in your life.

Now, that doesn't mean you can eat unhealthy foods all the time and expect to live healed and live long. Most sickness is self-induced by living wrong and eating wrong. There are natural and spiritual laws by which we are to live. It's our responsibility to eat the right kinds of food, exercise and rest—to make choices that will help us stay healthy.

Guard Your Heart

If symptoms linger, if our healing doesn't readily manifest, Ken and I start checking to see if we are walking in love and obeying God. We ask ourselves if we are spending enough time in the Word of God for it to be made life and health to our flesh.

Proverbs 4:23 in *The Amplified Bible* warns, "Keep and guard your heart with all vigilance and above all that you guard, for out of it flow the springs of life." You "keep" your heart by keeping it full of the Word of God. That's the most important thing you have to do in this life. You can't live in divine health and keep your faith up without a steady diet of the life force of God, which is the Word of God.

The wisdom of God is written down for us in His Word. Revelation of the Word is precious because it takes care of everything in our lives. It causes health and healing to come. It brings happiness, joy and peace—nothing missing, nothing broken. Walking in God's wisdom is a key to living long and living well. Proverbs 3:13-18 says:

Happy is the man that findeth wisdom, and the man that getteth understanding. For the merchandise of it is better than the merchandise of silver, and the gain thereof than fine gold. She is more precious than rubies: and all the things thou canst desire are not to be compared unto her. *Length of days* is in her right hand; and in her left hand riches and honour. Her ways are ways of pleasantness, and all her paths are peace. She is a *tree of life* to them that lay hold upon her: and happy is every one that retaineth her.

By spending time in the Word of God we can have so much life flowing out of us that sickness and disease can't even get close to us.

I'm convinced it would be possible to live to be 120 years old by obeying the Word of God. If you ate the way God said to eat and abstained from what He said to abstain from, you'd be well on your way to a strong, healthy body. Add to that a steady diet of the Word of God, allowing the Word to continually quicken (make alive) your mortal flesh.

Then if you were faithful to obey the Word of God in every area of life, I believe you could live an active, productive life of 120 years or more.

When you walk with God, you can walk healed and live long. "And ye shall serve the Lord your God, and he shall bless thy bread, and thy water; and I will take sickness away from the midst of thee...*the number of thy days I will fulfil*" (Exodus 23:25-26).

---

*The ArtScroll Tanach Series Tehillim/Psalms © 1977, 1985, by Mesorah Publications Ltd., www.artscroll.com

(From: "Live Long, Live Strong," the *Believer's Voice of Victory* magazine, April 2004 and various 2003 Kenneth Copeland Ministries' meetings)

Morning Reflection

How is walking in divine health better than being healed?

_____

_____

_____

_____

_____

_____

_____

How are eating right, exercise and rest important for a believer?

_____

_____

_____

_____

_____

_____

_____

What part does wisdom from the Word play in our health?

_____
_____
_____
_____
_____
_____
_____
_____
_____
_____

Today's Connection Points

- ● *Healing Praise* **CD: "Sing Hallelujah to the Lord," "Rise and Be Healed" (Tracks 11-12)**

  Give God praise as you let faith arise in your soul. Rise and be healed!

- ● *Healing Scriptures* **CD: Tracks 11-12**

  Take time out to get quiet as you revisit many of the healing scriptures we've covered in this study.

  1 Peter 2:24; 1 John 3:7-8; 3 John 2; Luke 6:6-10, 8:41-52, 54-56; Colossians 2:13-15

- ● **DVD: "God's Peace" (Chapter 10)**

  Receive God's peace as you hear about Christ's redemptive sacrifice for your healing!

Faith
in Action

 ### *Make a decision to operate in God's wisdom every day.*
Make eating right and exercising part of your new carefree life.

Notes:

_____
_____
_____
_____
_____
_____
_____
_____
_____
_____
_____
_____
_____
_____
_____
_____
_____
_____

Living Care Free
by Kenneth Copeland

Living a healthy life includes living free from worry and stress. But is that possible? When the bills come in, when your children are running wild through the house, when sickness is threatening and there's more laundry to do, is it possible to have a peaceful life?

Yes—and you don't have to leave the country to do it! No matter how intense or trivial the problems facing you are right now, you can live the most peaceful, carefree life you've ever lived—and you can start today.

How?

Look at 1 Peter 5:6-7 and I'll show you. It says, "Humble yourselves therefore under the mighty hand of God, that he may exalt you in due time: casting all your care upon him; for he careth for you."

As a believer, you're probably familiar with that scripture. But have you ever taken it seriously enough to put it into action? There's a good chance you haven't because you haven't understood just how dangerous those cares you're carrying around actually are. You probably haven't realized they are a deadly part of the devil's strategy against you.

That's right. Worry is one of the chief weapons of his warfare. If he can get you to worry about them, he can use the financial and family pressures and scheduling problems that are just a "normal" part of everyday life to weigh you down, drain your spiritual strength and drag you into more sickness and trouble than you care to think about.

You see, worry produces a deadly force: fear. It's what Satan uses to govern his kingdom. He uses it to steal, kill and destroy. Fear kills.

That's why all through the Bible the Holy Spirit commands, "Fear not!" He's not just giving friendly advice. He's giving us an order from our Commander in Chief, an order that will keep us from falling prey to the enemy's attack.

Medical science tells us that approximately 80 percent of the people hospitalized in the United States are there with ailments caused by worry and tension. Yet a great many believers worry without even thinking about it.

They'll worry about finding the time to get their hair cut. They'll worry about getting the right present for Grandma's birthday. They'll stew over this and that, and then go to church and not even realize they've been sinning all week long!

"Sinning, Brother Copeland?"

Yes! For the born-again, Spirit-filled

believer who owns a Bible—worrying is a sin.

I've had people say to me, "Brother Copeland, pray for me that I'll be able to bear these burdens." Well, I won't do it. Jesus said if you're burdened and heavy-laden, to come to Him and He'd give you rest. He didn't say, "Pray and I'll give you the strength to bear your burdens." He said, "I'll give you rest!"

Let's get something straight right now. A mind that is burdened down with worry is not a godly mind. You may be born again and baptized in the Holy Spirit, but if your mind is controlled by worry it is not controlled by the Holy Spirit.

I don't care how major or minor your problem is; Philippians 4:6 says to be anxious about nothing, but in everything pray and give thanks and make your requests known to God. It doesn't say, "Worry about it for four or five days." It says, "Pray and give thanks."

That means if you're going to obey God, you must make a decision to quit worrying. You must realize that it's part of Satan's strategy.

Speak the Word

"But what should I do with my cares," you say, "if I'm not going to worry about them anymore?"

You use the force of faith and do just what Jesus did when the devil came at Him.

Jesus said, "The prince of this world cometh, and hath nothing in me" (John 14:30). The devil never could get any of his junk into Jesus. He threw at Him everything he could throw, but Jesus wouldn't let it in.

He'd just say, "No, I don't live by that. I live by the Word, thank you." He wouldn't receive anything the devil said. He just trusted God and said, "It is written...."

When the devil attacked Jesus with worry, He didn't give in to it. He fought back with His double-edged sword. He clobbered the devil with the Spirit-power of the Word.

You see, the only way you can truly cast your care on God is by believing what He's already said about that care. The only way you can be free when it comes to finances is by believing that God has met all your needs according to His riches in glory by Christ Jesus (Philippians 4:19). The only way you can cast the care of sickness over on God is by believing that by His stripes you were healed (1 Peter 2:24).

That's why, when the devil wants to destroy you, he'll send a demon spirit to exalt himself against the Word of God. If you're sick, he'll begin to tell you, "You're not healed. You know healing is not for today. Even if it were, it wouldn't work for you. It might for someone else, but not you."

When he starts to tell you that kind of thing, don't buy into it! Don't start worrying around about it and thinking, *Oh my, I'm afraid I'm not going to get healed. I sure don't feel healed. I'm probably just going to get worse and worse....*

Don't do that! Do as Paul said in 2 Co-rinthians 10:5: "Casting down imaginations, and every high thing that exalteth itself against the knowledge of God, and bringing into captivity every thought...." Hit the devil with the Word, and cast the care of the situation over on God.

If you're thinking, *Yes, that sounds like a good thing to do, but I'm not Jesus! I'm just little old me,* remember that Jesus said He wasn't the One responsible for His success. He was using the Word of God. He said, "The Father that dwelleth in me, he doeth the works" (John 14:10).

Remember that. It's the Word that does the work, not the one holding on to it. It'll work for anyone who will put it to work. It will work for you just like it worked for Jesus. Just put it out there, and then get in behind it and hide. Let the Word fight its own fight.

God Will Lift You Up

Once, when I was preaching in Louisiana, it was the last night of the meeting and the budget hadn't been met. We were $900 short. During those early days, $900 might as well have been $9 million.

The devil was jumping on me so bad I couldn't afford to let my mind run loose five seconds. So I went outside and started walking up and down the motel patio, praising the Lord out loud. I'd found that my tongue controlled my mind.

By the way, if you haven't discovered that, let me demonstrate it really quickly. Start counting silently from one to 10. Now, while you're still counting, say your name out loud. See what I mean? Your head had to stop counting and see what your mouth had to say, didn't it? Use that the next time your mind starts to worry about something. Make it stop by speaking the promises of God out loud.

Anyway, I was walking back and forth out there, praying out loud, confessing the Word and praising God. Whenever I'd stop, the devil would say, "You ain't going to get it."

Then, I'd say, "As far as I'm concerned I already have it. I prayed and cast that care over on God, and He pays His bills!"

I just kept it up and kept it up, holding the devil over in the arena of faith, rather than letting him pull me over in to that arena of worry.

Suddenly a man pulled up into the motel driveway. He honked his horn and stuck his head out the window. "Brother Copeland, I'm so glad I caught you. I had to get by here to see you because I won't get to the meeting until late tonight and I was afraid I might miss the offering."

He held out a check and said, "I wanted to make sure you got this." Then he turned around and drove off. The check was for $500. That night we went over the budget.

You see, God will handle it for you if you cast those cares on Him. Not only that, but He also says He'll exalt you. Exalt you above what? Above the devil and all his crowd. Above every problem he tries to use against you.

That's God's plan for your victory. It doesn't make Him any difference if it's December or the Fourth of July. It doesn't matter if the dog needs a bath, *again,* and everyone on your son's soccer team is coming to your house for dinner. The Bible says, "...delight thyself in the Lord; and I will cause thee to ride upon the high places of the earth" (Isaiah 58:14).

God is an exalter. He wants to lift you above that anxiety and care the devil uses to pull you down. You can understand now why the psalmist says, "He maketh my feet like hinds' feet..." (Psalm 18:33). A deer's feet touch the ground every once in a while, but most of the time, they're in the air!

Now, go ahead and have a truly peaceful—and truly healed—life, you carefree thing, you!

(From: *One Word From God Can Change Your Health* by Kenneth and Gloria Copeland © 1999 Kenneth and Gloria Copeland)

Evening Reflection

Why is worrying a sin?

_____
_____
_____
_____
_____
_____
_____

When the enemy approaches you with worry, how should you respond?

_____
_____
_____
_____
_____
_____

What will you do to rise above anxiety today?

_____
_____
_____
_____
_____
_____
_____

Notes:

_____

_____

_____

_____

_____

_____

_____

_____

_____

_____

_____

_____

_____

_____

_____

_____

_____

_____

_____

_____

_____

_____

_____

Today's
Prayer of Faith

I choose to stand firm in Your peace, Father. You are my peace. Thank You for helping me walk by faith and not by sight. I have confidence in Your Word and I know that the work You started in me, You are completing. Thank You, Father. In Jesus' Name. Amen.

_____
_____
_____
_____
_____
_____
_____
_____
_____

I Will Never Leave You

My wife and I have been watching your program, *Believer's Voice of Victory,* for years and we have been extremely blessed. You and your guests have covered many topics that have really hit home. In February 2005, I was taken to the hospital by ambulance because I could not use my right leg. I was very weak and could barely stand. Once there, they did an ultrasound and found a blood clot the size of a golf ball. They admitted me and did surgery two hours later.

After several more tests, it was determined that I had malignant cancer. The following Monday I had surgery. After I awoke from the surgery, one of the doctors said with a gloomy face, "You know what we found in there, don't you?"

I said, with a smile, "Yes, you found malignant cancer, so what do you want me to do about it?" I had no fear at all. I knew what the Word of God said and that was all I needed. That Wednesday I started chemotherapy. The chemo dropped my white blood cell count from 10,000 to 0. I was so weak that I could hardly hold my head up. I was watching a monitor and looking at how good my blood pressure was. All of a sudden, it crashed down to 77/44. I knew from the medical training I had, that I was in the danger zone of going into cardiac arrest, but I didn't. I told a nurse that I couldn't breathe. The last thing I remember, they were rushing me to ICU, where I spent the next three and a half weeks on a respirator. They kept telling my wife to call all my family, that I most likely wouldn't make it through another night. But my God had other plans.

After I woke up from the coma, I heard the Lord speak to my spirit. He said, *I will never leave you nor forsake you!* That ministered to me. When I was able to turn on the television, the first program I saw was *Believer's Voice of Victory.* God healed everything the devil had tried to steal!

G.L.
Texas

Through your use of all the LifeLine materials, in what three areas has your faith grown the most?

1. _____

2. _____

3. _____

What are three ways you are now putting your faith into action?

1. _____

2. _____

3. _____

As your faith has grown, what are three ways you can be a blessing to others this week?

1. _____

2. _____

3. _____

Appendix A
Prayers and Confessions
Based on God's Word

These can also be found on your Faith in Action Cards.

1. Philippians 1:6

I am convinced and sure that He who began a good work in me will continue until the day of Jesus Christ, developing and perfecting and bringing it to full completion in me.

2. John 10:10

The thief comes only to steal and kill and destroy. You came, Lord, that I may have and enjoy life, and have it in abundance (to the full, till it overflows).

3. Isaiah 53:4-5

You, Lord, have taken my griefs (sicknesses, weaknesses and distresses) and carried my sorrows and pains. You were wounded for my transgression, bruised for my guilt and iniquities; the chastisement needed for my peace and well-being was upon You, Jesus, and by Your stripes I am healed and made whole.

4. Psalm 103:2-5

I gratefully praise You, Lord, and do not forget all Your benefits. You forgive all my iniquities and heal all my diseases. You redeem my life from the pit and corruption. You beautify, dignify and crown me with loving kindness and tender mercy.

5. Proverbs 4:20-23

I attend to God's Word and submit to His sayings. I will keep them in my sight, and in the center of my heart. They are life to me, and healing to my whole body.

6. Psalm 91:9-10, 14-16

Because I have made You, Lord, my refuge, and the Most High my dwelling place, there shall no evil befall me, nor any plague or calamity come near my house. Because I have set my love on You, Lord, therefore You deliver me. You set me securely on high, because I have known Your Name. I call upon You, Lord, and You answer me. You, Father, are with me in trouble. You deliver and honor me. With long life You will satisfy me and show me Your salvation.

7. 2 Timothy 1:7

God has not given me a spirit of timidity and fear. He has given me a spirit of power and of love and of a calm and well-balanced mind, discipline and self-control.

8. Isaiah 40:29, 31

You give power to me when I am faint and weary. In my weakness, You increase strength in me. I wait for You [expect, look for and hope in You] and You renew my strength and power. I will lift up with wings of strength and rise as an eagle. I shall run and not be weary, I shall walk and not faint or become tired.

9. 2 Corinthians 10:3-5

Even though I have a physical body, I will not carry on warfare according to the flesh, using mere human weapons. The weapons of my warfare are not physical (weapons of flesh and blood), they are mighty before God for the overthrow and destruction of strongholds. I refute arguments and theories and reasonings and every proud and lofty thing that sets itself up against the true knowledge of God; and I lead every thought and purpose away captive into the obedience of Christ.

10. Philippians 4:6-7

I will not fret or have anxiety about anything, but in every circumstance and in everything, by prayer and petition, with thanksgiving, continue to make my requests known to God. God's peace which transcends all understanding, shall garrison and mount guard over my heart and mind in Christ Jesus.

Appendix B
Healing Scriptures

Healing
Scriptures

The following scriptures have helped us get healed, and stay healed, again and again. Read them continually to keep your faith for healing high. Most of them originated from a list made by Dodie Osteen, who was healed of terminal liver cancer many years ago. She took them daily like medicine, until every symptom was gone, and still takes them every day to maintain divine health.

"To be spoken by mouth three times a day until faith comes, then once a day to maintain faith. If circumstances grow worse, double the dosage. There are no harmful side effects."

—Charles Capps

Exodus 15:26

If thou wilt diligently hearken to the voice of the Lord thy God, and wilt do that which is right in his sight, and wilt give ear to his commandments, and keep all his statutes, I will put none of these diseases upon thee, which I have brought upon the Egyptians: for I am the Lord that healeth thee.

Exodus 23:25-26

And ye shall serve the Lord your God, and he shall bless thy bread, and thy water; and I will take sickness away from the midst of thee. There shall nothing cast their young, nor be barren, in thy land: the number of thy days I will fulfil.

Deuteronomy 7:14-15

Thou shalt be blessed above all people: there shall not be male or female barren among you, or among your cattle. And the Lord will take away from thee all sickness, and will put none of the evil diseases of Egypt, which thou knowest, upon thee; but will lay them upon all them that hate thee.

Deuteronomy 30:19-20

I call heaven and earth to record this day against you, that I have set before you life and death, blessing and cursing: therefore choose life, that both thou and thy seed may live: That thou mayest love the Lord thy God, and that thou mayest obey his voice, and that thou mayest cleave unto him: for he is thy life, and the length of thy days: that thou mayest dwell in the land which the Lord sware unto thy fathers, to Abraham, to Isaac, and to Jacob, to give them.

1 Kings 8:56

Blessed be the Lord, that hath given rest unto his people Israel, according to all that he promised: there hath not failed one word of all his good promise, which he promised by the hand of Moses his servant.

Psalm 91:9-10, 14-16

Because thou hast made the Lord, which is my refuge, even the most High, thy habitation; there shall no evil befall thee, neither shall any plague come nigh thy dwelling.

Because he hath set his love upon me, therefore will I deliver him: I will set him on high, because he hath known my name. He shall call upon me, and I will answer him: I will be with him in trouble; I will deliver him, and honour him. With long life will I satisfy him, and show him my salvation.

Psalm 103:1-5

Bless the Lord, O my soul: and all that is within me, bless his holy name. Bless the Lord, O my soul, and forget not all his benefits: who forgiveth all thine iniquities; who healeth all thy diseases; who redeemeth thy life from destruction; who crowneth thee with lovingkindness and tender mercies; who satisfieth thy mouth with good things; so that thy youth is renewed like the eagle's.

Psalm 107:17, 19-21

Fools because of their transgression, and because of their iniquities, are afflicted.

Then they cry unto the Lord in their trouble, and he saveth them out of their distresses. He sent his word, and healed them, and delivered them from their destructions. Oh that men would praise the Lord for his goodness, and for his wonderful works to the children of men!

Psalm 118:17

I shall not die, but live, and declare the works of the Lord.

Proverbs 4:20-24

My son, attend to my words; incline thine ear unto my sayings. Let them not depart from thine eyes; keep them in the midst of thine heart. For they are life unto those that find them, and health to all their flesh. Keep thy heart with all diligence; for out of it are the issues of life. Put away from thee a froward mouth, and perverse lips put far from thee.

Isaiah 41:10

Fear thou not; for I am with thee: be not dismayed; for I am thy God: I will strengthen thee; yea, I will help thee; yea, I will uphold thee with the right hand of my righteousness.

Isaiah 53:4-5

Surely he hath borne our griefs, and carried our sorrows: yet we did esteem him stricken, smitten of God, and afflicted. But he was wounded for our transgressions, he was bruised for our iniquities: the chastisement of our peace was upon him; and with his stripes we are healed.

Jeremiah 1:12

Then said the Lord unto me, Thou hast well seen: for I will hasten my word to perform it.

Jeremiah 17:14

Heal me, O Lord, and I shall be healed; save me, and I shall be saved: for thou art my praise.

Jeremiah 30:17

For I will restore health unto thee, and I will heal thee of thy wounds, saith the Lord.

Joel 3:10

Beat your ploughshares into swords, and your pruning hooks into spears: let the weak say, I am strong.

Nahum 1:9

What do ye imagine against the Lord? he will make an utter end: affliction shall not rise up the second time.

Matthew 8:2-3

And, behold, there came a leper and worshipped him, saying, Lord, if thou wilt, thou canst make me clean. And Jesus put forth his hand, and touched him, saying, I will; be thou clean. And immediately his leprosy was cleansed.

Matthew 8:16-17

When the even was come, they brought unto him many that were possessed with devils: and he cast out the spirits with his word, and healed all that were sick: that it might be fulfilled which was spoken by Esaias the prophet, saying, Himself took our infirmities, and bare our sicknesses.

Matthew 15:30-31

And great multitudes came unto him, having with them those that were lame, blind, dumb, maimed, and many others, and cast them down at Jesus' feet; and he healed them: insomuch that the multitude wondered, when they saw the dumb to speak, the maimed to be whole, the lame to walk, and the blind to see: and they glorified the God of Israel.

Matthew 18:18-19

Verily I say unto you, Whatsoever ye shall bind on earth shall be bound in heaven: and whatsoever ye shall loose on earth shall be loosed in heaven. Again I say unto you, That if two of you shall agree on earth as touching any thing that they shall ask, it shall be done for them of my Father which is in heaven.

Matthew 21:21-22

Jesus answered and said unto them, Verily I say unto you, If ye have faith, and doubt not, ye shall not only do this which is done to the fig tree, but also if ye shall say unto this mountain, Be thou removed, and be thou cast into the sea; it shall be done. And all things, whatsoever ye shall ask in prayer, believing, ye shall receive.

Mark 9:23

Jesus said unto him, If thou canst believe, all things are possible to him that believeth.

Mark 10:27

And Jesus looking upon them saith, With men it is impossible, but not with God: for with God all things are possible.

Mark 11:22-24

And Jesus answering saith unto them, Have faith in God. For verily I say unto you, That whosoever shall say unto this mountain, Be thou removed, and be thou cast into the sea; and shall not doubt in his heart, but shall believe that those things which he saith shall come to pass; he shall have whatsoever he saith. Therefore I say unto you, What things soever ye desire, when ye pray, believe that ye receive them, and ye shall have them.

Mark 16:14-18

Afterward he appeared unto the eleven as they sat at meat, and upbraided them with their unbelief and hardness of heart, because they believed not them which had seen him after he was risen. And he said unto them, Go ye into all the world, and preach the gospel to every creature. He that believeth and is baptized shall be saved; but he that believeth not shall be damned. And these signs shall follow them that believe; In my name shall they cast out devils; they shall speak with new tongues; they shall take up serpents; and if they drink any deadly thing, it shall not hurt them; they shall lay hands on the sick, and they shall recover.

Luke 6:19

And the whole multitude sought to touch him: for there went virtue out of him, and healed them all.

Luke 9:2

And he sent them to preach the kingdom of God, and to heal the sick.

Luke 13:16

And ought not this woman, being a daughter of Abraham, whom Satan hath bound, lo, these eighteen years, be loosed from this bond on the sabbath day?

Acts 5:16

There came also a multitude out of the cities round about unto Jerusalem, bringing sick folks, and them which were vexed with unclean spirits: and they were healed every one.

Acts 10:38

How God anointed Jesus of Nazareth with the Holy Ghost and with power: who went about doing good, and healing all that were oppressed of the devil; for God was with him.

Romans 4:16-21

Therefore it is of faith, that it might be by grace; to the end the promise might be sure to all the seed; not to that only which is of the law, but to that also which is of the faith of Abraham; who is the father of us all, (as it is written, I have made thee a father of many nations,) before him whom he believed, even God, who quickeneth the dead, and calleth those things which be not as though they were. Who against hope believed in hope, that he might become the father of many nations, according to that which was spoken, So shall thy seed be. And being not weak in faith, he considered not his own body now dead, when he was about an hundred years old, neither yet the deadness of Sarah's womb: He staggered not at the promise of God through unbelief; but was strong in faith, giving glory to God; and being fully persuaded that, what he had promised, he was able also to perform.

Romans 8:2, 11

For the law of the Spirit of life in Christ Jesus hath made me free from the law of sin and death.

But if the Spirit of him that raised up Jesus from the dead dwell in you, he that raised up Christ from the dead shall also quicken your mortal bodies by his Spirit that dwelleth in you.

2 Corinthians 4:18

While we look not at the things which are seen, but at the things which are not seen: for the things which are seen are temporal; but the things which are not seen are eternal.

2 Corinthians 10:3-5

For though we walk in the flesh, we do not war after the flesh: (For the weapons of our warfare are not carnal, but mighty through God to the pulling down of strong holds;) casting down imaginations, and every high thing that exalteth itself against the knowledge of God, and bringing into captivity every thought to the obedience of Christ.

Galatians 3:13-14, 29

Christ hath redeemed us from the curse of the law, being made a curse for us: for it is written, Cursed is every one that hangeth on a tree: that the blessing of Abraham might come on the Gentiles through Jesus Christ; that we might receive the promise of the Spirit through faith.

And if ye be Christ's, then are ye Abraham's seed, and heirs according to the promise.

Ephesians 6:10-17

Finally, my brethren, be strong in the Lord, and in the power of his might. Put on the whole armour of God, that ye may be able to stand against the wiles of the devil. For we wrestle not against flesh and blood, but against principalities, against powers, against the rulers of the darkness of this world, against spiritual wickedness in high places. Wherefore take unto you the whole armour of God, that ye may be able to withstand in the evil day, and having done all, to stand. Stand therefore, having your loins girt about with truth, and having on the breastplate of righteousness; and your feet shod with the preparation of the gospel of peace; above all, taking the shield of faith, wherewith ye shall be able to quench all the fiery darts of the wicked. And take the helmet of salvation, and the sword of the Spirit, which is the word of God.

Philippians 2:13

[Not in your own strength] for it is God Who is all the while effectually at work in you [energizing and creating in you the power and desire], both to will and to work for His good pleasure and satisfaction and delight. *(The Amplified Bible)*

Philippians 4:6-9

Do not fret or have any anxiety about anything, but in every circumstance and in everything, by prayer and petition (definite requests), with thanksgiving, continue to make your wants known to God. And God's peace [shall be yours, that tranquil state of a soul assured of its salvation through Christ, and so fearing nothing from God and being content with its earthly lot of whatever sort that is, that peace] which transcends all understanding shall garrison and mount guard over your hearts and minds in Christ Jesus. For the rest, brethren, whatever is true, whatever is worthy of reverence and is honorable and seemly, whatever is just, whatever is pure, whatever is lovely and lovable, whatever is kind and winsome and gracious, if there is any virtue and excellence, if there is anything worthy of praise, think on and weigh and take account of these things [fix your minds on them]. Practice what you have learned and received and heard and seen in me, and model your way of living on it, and the God of peace (of untroubled, undisturbed well-being) will be with you. *(The Amplified Bible)*

2 Timothy 1:7

For God hath not given us the spirit of fear; but of power, and of love, and of a sound mind.

Hebrews 10:23

Let us hold fast the profession of our faith without wavering; (for he is faithful that promised).

Hebrews 10:35-36

Cast not away therefore your confidence, which hath great recompence of reward. For ye have need of patience, that, after ye have done the will of God, ye might receive the promise.

Hebrews 11:11

Through faith also Sarah herself received strength to conceive seed, and was delivered of a child when she was past age, because she judged him faithful who had promised.

Hebrews 13:8

Jesus Christ the same yesterday, and today, and for ever.

James 4:7

Submit yourselves therefore to God. Resist the devil, and he will flee from you.

James 5:14-16

Is any sick among you? let him call for the elders of the church; and let them pray over him, anointing him with oil in the name of the Lord: And the prayer of faith shall save the sick, and the Lord shall raise him up; and if he have committed sins, they shall be forgiven him. Confess your faults one to another, and pray one for another, that ye may be healed. The effectual fervent prayer of a righteous man availeth much.

1 Peter 2:24

Who his own self bare our sins in his own body on the tree, that we, being dead to sins, should live unto righteousness: by whose stripes ye were healed.

1 John 3:21-22

Beloved, if our heart condemn us not, then have we confidence toward God. And whatsoever we ask, we receive of him, because we keep his commandments, and do those things that are pleasing in his sight.

1 John 5:14-15

And this is the confidence that we have in him, that, if we ask any thing according to his will, he heareth us: And if we know that he hear us, whatsoever we ask, we know that we have the petitions that we desired of him.

3 John 2

Beloved, I wish above all things that thou mayest prosper and be in health, even as thy soul prospereth.

Revelation 12:11

And they overcame him by the blood of the Lamb, and by the word of their testimony; and they loved not their lives unto the death.

Appendix C
LifeLine Healing
Prayer Guide

LifeLine Healing
Prayer Guide

Part of the purpose of the LifeLine kits is to give you an "at-your-fingertips" resource to help you pray for yourself and others. Use this handy, practical guide as a starting point for power-filled prayer to change things in your life and the lives of others as you connect with God through His Word.

In addition to the scriptures we have been studying in this LifeLine kit, the New Testament has many examples of believers praying for healing for those around them. In fact, we are encouraged to pray for healing for one another.

As you pray, remember to boldly confess the scriptures over each situation. Your scripture action cards are an excellent resource for healing scriptures and, of course, your Bible, where you'll find many more!

Praying for Others—General

What does God's Word say?

James 5:14-15:

Is anyone among you sick? He should call in the church elders (the spiritual guides). And they should pray over him, anointing him with oil in the Lord's name. And the prayer [that is] of faith will save him who is sick, and the Lord will restore him; and if he has committed sins, he will be forgiven. *(The Amplified Bible)*

Here is an example of how you can pray for others:

Father, it is Your will for us to walk in health. Thank You for providing health and healing for us through the shed blood of Jesus on the cross. According to Your Word I release my faith and speak healing and life to this precious person. I rebuke sickness and disease and command it to leave _____'s body, now, in the Name of Jesus. I speak total restoration to him/her, spirit, soul and body. In Jesus' Name. Amen.

Praying for Your Children

What does God's Word say?

In 1 Corinthians 7:14, we see that in God's eyes, our children are holy, even if one parent is not a believer:

> For the unbelieving husband has been sanctified through his wife, and the unbelieving wife has been sanctified through her believing husband. Otherwise your children would be unclean, but as it is, they are holy. *(New International Version)*

How did Jesus demonstrate the heart of our heavenly Father?

Matthew 19:13-14:

> Then little children were brought to Jesus, that He might put His hands on them and pray; but the disciples rebuked those who brought them. But He said, Leave the children alone! Allow the little ones to come to Me, and do not forbid or restrain or hinder them, for of such [as these] is the kingdom of heaven composed. *(The Amplified Bible)*

Here is an example of how you can pray for your children:

Father, I am so grateful to know how You love _____ and see him/her as holy! Thank You for showing _____ Your love through our Lord Jesus Christ, who took sickness and disease on Himself for _____. According to Your Word in 1 Peter 2:24 that says by Your stripes _____ was healed, I speak healing and life to _____'s body. I rebuke sickness and disease from off him/her and I speak total restoration to _____, spirit, soul and body, in the Name of Jesus. I declare that Jesus is Lord of this home! Amen.

Notes:

_____
_____
_____
_____
_____
_____
_____
_____
_____
_____
_____

Praying for Your Friends

What does God's Word say?

James 5:16

Confess to one another therefore your faults (your slips, your false steps, your offenses, your sins) and pray [also] for one another, that you may be healed and restored [to a spiritual tone of mind and heart]. The earnest (heartfelt, continued) prayer of a righteous man makes tremendous power available [dynamic in its working] *(The Amplified Bible)*.

How did Jesus demonstrate the heart of our heavenly Father?

In Luke 5:18-20, 25, we see the power of faith-filled friends!

> And behold, some men were bringing on a stretcher a man who was paralyzed, and they tried to carry him in and lay him before [Jesus]. But finding no way to bring him in because of the crowd, they went up on the roof and lowered him with his stretcher through the tiles into the midst, in front of Jesus. And when He saw [their confidence in Him, springing from] their faith, He said, Man, your sins are forgiven you!... And instantly [the man] stood up before them and picked up what he had been lying on and went away to his house, recognizing and praising and thanking God *(The Amplified Bible)*.

Here is an example of how you can pray for your friends:

As the Body of Christ we share in each others' lives, and follow the example of our Lord Jesus, as we pray for each other. Thank You, Father, that You are the author of every good thing, including the compassion we share as friends. Thank You for proving Your love and power through the death and resurrection of our Lord Jesus Christ, who took sickness and disease on Himself for us. According to Your Word in Matthew 18:18-19, Isaiah 53:4-5 and 1 Peter 2:24, we stand in agreement as we lay hands on _____.
We rebuke sickness and disease off his/her body and declare he/she is made whole, spirit, soul and body, in the Name of Jesus. Amen.

Praying for Yourself

What does God's Word say?

1 John 5:14-15:

This is the confidence we have in approaching God: that if we ask anything according to his will, he hears us. And if we know that he hears us—whatever we ask—we know that we have what we asked of him. *(New International Version)*

How did Jesus demonstrate the heart of our heavenly Father?

In Mark 10:46-52 we see how Jesus responded to Bartimaeus, who was blind. Take note of how important it was for Bartimaeus to come to Jesus to ask:

Then they came to Jericho. And as He was leaving Jericho with His disciples and a great crowd, Bartimaeus, a blind beggar, a son of Timaeus, was sitting by the roadside. And when he heard that it was Jesus of Nazareth, he began to shout, saying, Jesus, Son of David, have pity and mercy on me [now]! And many severely censured and reproved him, telling him to keep still, but he kept on shouting out all the more, You Son of David, have pity and mercy on me [now]! And Jesus stopped and said, Call him. And they called the blind man, telling him, Take courage! Get up! He is calling you. And throwing off his outer garment, he leaped up and came to Jesus. And Jesus said to him, What do you want Me to do for you? And the blind man said to Him, Master, let me receive my sight. And Jesus said to him, Go your way; your faith has healed you. And at once he received his sight and accompanied Jesus on the road. *(The Amplified Bible)*

Here is an example of how you can pray for yourself:

Thank You, Father, for showing me Your character and will through Your written Word, and through the Living Word, my Lord Jesus Christ. I come to You now, confident of Your desire for my total health. Your Word says in Exodus 15:26 that You are the Lord who heals me. You said in Isaiah 53:4-5 that You took my infirmities and bore my sicknesses and by Your stripes I am healed. When You were in Your earthly ministry, You healed all who came to You. And You said in 1 Peter 2:24 that because of Your shed blood on the Cross, by Your stripes I was already healed. So I take courage and declare by faith according to Your Word, that by Your stripes I am healed, now! I believe I receive my healing in the Name of Jesus. I receive Your strength and as I go my way, walking with You, I believe Your Anointing is working mightily in me. Thank You, Lord, in Jesus' Name. Amen.

Dear Friend,

We are standing with you, believing God for His very best for every area of your life…and that includes your complete prosperity!

You may have finished this book, but don't let that be the end of your journey. Keep meditating on the truths you've learned. Listen to the CDs often, watch the DVD again and constantly keep the Word before your eyes. As you do, you can rest in the knowledge that God's Word always accomplishes what it was sent to do (Isaiah 55:11).

Then, when your breakthrough comes—and we believe it *will* come if it hasn't already—please contact us and let us know so that we may rejoice with you. Praise God, we're believing for good news from the top of the world to the bottom and all the way around…and we're thrilled you're part of it!

JESUS IS LORD!

Kenneth & Gloria Copeland

Prayer for Salvation and Baptism
in the Holy Spirit

Heavenly Father, I come to You in the Name of Jesus. Your Word says, "Whosoever shall call on the name of the Lord shall be saved" (Acts 2:21). I am calling on You. I pray and ask Jesus to come into my heart and be Lord over my life according to Romans 10:9-10: "If thou shalt confess with thy mouth the Lord Jesus, and shalt believe in thine heart that God hath raised him from the dead, thou shalt be saved. For with the heart man believeth unto righteousness; and with the mouth confession is made unto salvation." I do that now. I confess that Jesus is Lord, and I believe in my heart that God raised Him from the dead.

I am now reborn! I am a Christian—a child of Almighty God! I am saved! You also said in Your Word, "If ye then, being evil, know how to give good gifts unto your children: HOW MUCH MORE shall your heavenly Father give the Holy Spirit to them that ask him?" (Luke 11:13). I'm also asking You to fill me with the Holy Spirit. Holy Spirit, rise up within me as I praise God. I fully expect to speak with other tongues as You give me the utterance (Acts 2:4). In Jesus' Name. Amen!

Begin to praise God for filling you with the Holy Spirit. Speak those words and syllables you receive—not in your own language, but the language given to you by the Holy Spirit. You have to use your own voice. God will not force you to speak. Don't be concerned with how it sounds. It is a heavenly language!

Continue with the blessing God has given you and pray in the spirit every day.

You are a born-again, Spirit-filled believer. You'll never be the same!

Find a good church that boldly preaches God's Word and obeys it. Become part of a church family who will love and care for you as you love and care for them.

We need to be connected to each other. It increases our strength in God. It's God's plan for us.

Make it a habit to watch the *Believer's Voice of Victory* television broadcast and become a doer of the Word, who is blessed in his doing (James 1:22-25).

About the Authors

Kenneth and Gloria Copeland are the best-selling authors of more than 60 books. They have also co-authored numerous books including *Family Promises* and *From Faith to Faith—A Daily Guide to Victory*. As founders of Kenneth Copeland Ministries in Fort Worth, Texas, Kenneth and Gloria are in their 41st year of circling the globe with the uncompromised Word of God, preaching and teaching a lifestyle of victory for every Christian.

Their daily and Sunday *Believer's Voice of Victory* television broadcasts now air on more than 500 stations around the world, and their *Believer's Voice of Victory* magazine is distributed to more than 1 million believers worldwide. Their international prison ministry reaches an average of 60,000 new inmates every year and receives more than 17,000 pieces of correspondence each month. Their teaching materials can also be found on the World Wide Web. With offices and staff in the United States, Canada, England, Australia, South Africa and Ukraine, Kenneth and Gloria's teaching materials—books, magazines, audios and videos—have been translated into at least 22 languages to reach the world with the love of God.

Learn more about Kenneth Copeland Ministries by visiting our Web site at **www.kcm.org**

Other Products to Help You Receive Your Healing

Books by Gloria Copeland
*And Jesus Healed Them All
God's Prescription for Divine Health
God's Will for Your Healing
*Harvest of Health
Words That Heal (gift book with CD enclosed)

Audio Resources by Gloria Copeland
Be Made Whole—Live Long, Live Healthy
God Is a Good God
God Wants You Well
Healing Confessions (CD and minibook)
Healing School

DVD Resources by Gloria Copeland
Be Made Whole—Live Long, Live Healthy
Know Him As Healer

Books by Kenneth Copeland
*You Are Healed!

Books Co-Authored by Kenneth and Gloria Copeland
Healing Promises
One Word From God Can Change Your Health

Audio Resources by Kenneth Copeland
Healing—Is It God's Will?
Healing Scriptures
Taking Authority Over the Curse

Audio Resources by Kellie Copeland Swisher
And Jesus Healed Them All—Healing Praise for Your Children
And Jesus Healed Them All Tote
Children's Healing Confession Book and Music CD

*Available in Spanish

World Offices
Kenneth Copeland Ministries

For more information about KCM and our products,
please write to the office nearest you:

Kenneth Copeland Ministries
Fort Worth, TX 76192-0001

Kenneth Copeland
Locked Bag 2600
Mansfield Delivery Centre
QUEENSLAND 4122
AUSTRALIA

Kenneth Copeland
Post Office Box 15
BATH
BA1 3XN
U.K.

Kenneth Copeland
Private Bag X 909
FONTAINEBLEAU
2032
REPUBLIC OF
SOUTH AFRICA

Kenneth Copeland
PO Box 3111 STN LCD 1
Langley BC V3A 4R3
CANADA

Kenneth Copeland Ministries
Post Office Box 84
L'VIV 79000
UKRAINE

We're Here for You!

Believer's Voice of Victory Television Broadcast

Join Kenneth and Gloria Copeland and the *Believer's Voice of Victory* broadcasts Monday through Friday and on Sunday each week, and learn how faith in God's Word can take your life from ordinary to extraordinary. This teaching from God's Word is designed to get you where you want to be—*on top!*

You can catch the *Believer's Voice of Victory* broadcast on your local, cable or satellite channels.* Also available 24 hours on webcast at BVOV.TV.

  * Check your local listings for times and stations in your area.

Believer's Voice of Victory Magazine

Enjoy inspired teaching and encouragement from Kenneth and Gloria Copeland and guest ministers each month in the *Believer's Voice of Victory* magazine. Also included are real-life testimonies of God's miraculous power and divine intervention in the lives of people just like you!

It's more than just a magazine—it's a ministry.

To receive a FREE subscription to
Believer's Voice of Victory, write to:

Kenneth Copeland Ministries
Fort Worth, TX 76192-0001

Or call:

800-600-7395
(7 a.m.-5 p.m. CT)

Or visit our Web site at:

www.kcm.org

If you are writing from outside the U.S., please contact the KCM office nearest you. Addresses for all Kenneth Copeland Ministries offices are listed on the previous pages.